THE BOOK ON PODCASTING

An Insider's Guide to Recording Success

The Podcaster's Coach
Alexander Laurin

10-10-10
Publishing

THE BOOK ON PODCASTING
An Insider's Guide to Recording Success

www.TheBookOnPodcasting.com
Copyright © 2018 ALEXANDER LAURIN
ISBN-13: 978-1984117557
ISBN-10: 1984117556

Limits of Liability and Disclaimer of Warranty
The author and publisher shall not be liable for your misuse of the enclosed material. This book is strictly for informational and educational purposes only.

Warning – Disclaimer
The purpose of this book is to educate and entertain. The author and/or publisher do not guarantee that anyone following these techniques, suggestions, tips, ideas, or strategies will become successful. The author and/or publisher shall have neither liability nor responsibility to anyone with respect to any loss or damage caused, or alleged to be caused, directly or indirectly by the information contained in this book.

Medical Disclaimer
The medical or health information in this book is provided as an information resource only, and is not to be used or relied on for any diagnostic or treatment purposes. This information is not intended to be patient education, does not create any patient-physician relationship, and should not be used as a substitute for professional diagnosis and treatment.

Publisher
10-10- 10 Publishing
Markham, ON
Canada

Printed in Canada and the United States of America

Contents

Dedication

I dedicate this book to my mom, Nancy. She is an amazing lady, a wonderful role model, and the most supportive, #1 fan anyone could possibly have.

&

All of my Listeners.

Acknowledgements

I wish to thank the following people for helping and inspiring me. I am extremely grateful to all of the people who have been there for me, and have showed me the path to becoming a successful person:

- **Kim** – My wife is an amazing individual, and she has helped me stretch my ways of thinking. Thank you, hon.
- **Remy, Sophia, and Mani** – Wonderful children who will grow into caring and giving adults. They will make positive contributions to the world.
- My mom, My dad, **Charles, Neil, Steven, Linda, May, Kwokeen, Diana, Gloria, Liane, Shuana, Liam, Paul, Ian, Austin, Rick, Jenn, Nic, Justin, Noah, Morgan, Taylor, Albert, Nadia, Luca, Lilianna, Michel, Antoinette, Nadia, Jay, Anthony, Bryan, Greg, Lee, Ben,** and the rest of my extended family and friends.
- **The Raymond Aaron Group** – For all of the mentorship, along with the generous offering of awards for both my writing and podcasting. **Raymond Aaron** has played a huge role in my life.
- **Josh Naaman, Jesse Kahat, Joe, Steven Pacheco, Michael Howie, Bunmi Akinnusotu, Rachel Reese, Gary Leland, Dave Lee, Gordon Firemark, Heneka Watkis-Porter, Pavo, Ian Farrar, and Rob O'Donohue** – Amazing, kind Podcasters, who contributed to my book. Check them all out!
- **Les Brown** – One of my favorite speakers, whose words helped pick me up when I was feeling down.
- **Tony Robbins** – For inspiring me to use my strength and influence to help others.
- **Chris Anderson** – Owner of TED, and creator of the Sapling Foundation, whose amazing work helps others live powerful lives.

- **Real Estate Wealth Expo Toronto Organizers** – Day one on a high speed rocket!
- **Brian K. Smith, aka Lama Marut** – An excellent teacher, whom I feel a strong connection with. I am forever grateful to him and his podcast.
- **His Holiness, the 14th Dalai Lama, Lama Zopa Rinpoche, and Bhikshuni Thubten Chodron** – Great Teachers who are always there for me.
- **Dr. Randin Brons** – The best Coach Instructor on the planet.
- **Tom Bournakas** – The entrepreneur with the biggest heart I have ever met.
- **PK Subban** – Inspired my love for the Canadiens, and my first podcast. He excited me on ice, and moved me by his charity work.
- **Podcast Movement Founders (Gary Leland, Jarod Easley, Dan Franks, & Mitch Todd)** – The men responsible for strengthening and helping the entire podcast community with their wonderful conference, and tireless work.
- **Gary Leland** – Additional acknowledgment and thanks for helping me. Put March 1st on your calendar, and celebrate Gary Leland Day.
- **John Lee Dumas** - For his kindness and motivation as I have trekked down this part of entrepreneurial journey.
- **Cliff Ravenscraft & Daniel J Lewis** – Through their podcasts, I developed the strength and know-how to get started.
- **Jim Treliving, Arlene Dickinson, & David Chilton** – These Dragons became my role models for financial success and generosity.
- **William Shatner** – Both of us are from an area in Montreal called NDG (Notre-Dame-de-Grâce). It doesn't matter where you were born when you want to make a difference in other people's lives.
- **Marco, Ramona,** and the memory of **Dalia Mascarin** – Learning about the sacredness of life and death, at the Institute of Traditional Medicine, in Toronto, was one of my most profound experiences. Thank You.
- **Amy Archer & Dean Walters** – Health Care Ass Kickers.
- **Barb Phillips** – Thanandoula extraordinaire!

- **Grant Cardone** – He made selling, fun; and gave me direction when I was starting over.
- **Christina Eanes, Jon Buscall, Josh Naaman, Justin Williams, Dirk Primbs, Pablo Fuentes, Gary Leland, Rob Cressy, Craig Burgess, Jesse Kahat, Joe, Steven Pacheco, Giovanna Rossi, Tim Lewis, Kirk Griffin, Carole Sanek, Mike Peacock, Robert Ingalls, Ramona Rice, Civilla Morgan, Dale Wiley, Tawny Platis, Sean Douglas, Felix Montelara, Michael Howie, Dorena Rode, Bunmi Akinnusotu, Glenn Rubenstein, Sean Callanan, Lee Ann Hopkins, Joel Sharpton, Thomas Hornigold, Yann Ilunga, Christian Swain, Janessa Jaye Champagne, Rhoda Sommer, Matt Sanderson, Devlin Wilder, Robert Forto, Blake, Rachel Reese, Craig Garber, Annalisa Parent, Phil Primeau, Stephen Guerra, Pavo, Kurt Sasso, Ryan Regan, Kingsley Grant, Sheena Yap Chan, Ember, Jacob Shao, Mike Norris, Mike Howell, Daniel J Lewis, Abel Kay, Adela Mizrachi, David Garofalo, Dave Lee, Mark Tilsher, Michael Opoku, Brett Robbo, Tyler Kirby, Sam Kabert, Gordon Firemark, Heneka Watkis-Porter, Cesar Zamudio, Randy Wilburn, Jeremy Enns, Bryan Entzminger, Ian Farrar, Eric Rosenberg, Matt Miller, Mark Deal, John Ashton, Anna Jaworski, Steve Stewart, Rob O'Donohue, Spiritual Homegirl, Austin Rumbaugh, Martin Landeskog, and Michael Woodword** – All of my great guests on *The Podcaster's Life.*
- **Sergio La Rosa & Marco Pracucci** – A great help during my podcast technical journey.
- **Marlon Shaw** – The amazing Speaker's Coach who made my life and presentations easy.
- **Afshin Mousavian, Lisa Trudeau, Jeff Lohnes, Dalia Haimen, Emma Truax, Laura Carinci, Kirstin Turnbull, Karun Malik, Catherine Fournier, and Janet Park** – The excellent TedX Toronto team that has tirelessly organized this wonderful event, which I have found of great value.
- **Dorena Rode** – My beta-reader who excels at planting very good seeds.

- **Tara Graham** - For the headshot on the back cover. She was wonderful and easy to work with.
- **Jean Guy St-Pierre** – The best accountant in Durham Region who has saved me a lot of money.
- **Katherine** – The lovely lady who poured all of the coffee I drank while writing this book.
- The Whitby Chamber of Commerce (**Natalie Prychitko, Brenda Bemis, Heather Bulman, Greg Frankson, Samantha Wallace, and Rylie Wilton**) – **A wonderful organization that I first joined in 2011, filled with great people who support local businesses in our beautiful town.**
- Business Advisory Centre Durham (**Teresa Shaver, Patrice Esper, Andrea Rowland, Ashley McBride, Bryan Kanarens, and Lindy Schultz**) – **Wonderful people offering wonderful resources to businesses and aspiring entrepreneurs in our Region.**
- **Albert Laurin** – Thanks cuz, for being there with me, right at the very beginning of this amazing ride that I am on.

About Alexander, The Podcaster's Coach

Alexander is the world's first authentic Certified Podcaster's Coach, which puts him at the forefront of Life Transformation within the podcast world. He was awarded Success Writer & Podcaster of the Year 2017 by New York Times Bestselling Author, Raymond Aaron.

A practicing member of the International Coaching Federation (ICF) and Certified Professional Life Coach, Alexander offers 'Podcast Success Coaching' for podcasters. He also helps consultants and aspiring entrepreneurs create podcast content marketing strategies for their businesses.

As part of his mission, he travels across the world conducting 'Podcast and Success Talks.' He delivers inspiration and life transformation strategies, and shows audiences the power of podcasting as a tool for success.

With *The Book on Podcasting*, he shares his experience of personal reinvention, positive change, and living a balanced life infused with purpose and fun. Inside are ideas to use the momentum of podcast creation to create a new awareness of purpose, meaning, self-care and community.

Alexander is the host of The Work Utopia Podcast, The Podcaster's Life, and The Micro Podcast Improv. These shows promote living with purpose, positive actions, personal achievement, humor, and of course, podcasts. Alexander also owns and operates Business Podcast Network.

When he's not traveling or working on his mission, Alexander lives in Whitby, Ontario, Canada, with his wife, Kim, and their three children.

For Coaching, Speaking, or to register for the 'Startup Podcast Program,' please visit www.podcasterscoach.com.

Foreword
By Raymond Aaron

I first spoke to Alexander Laurin, The Podcaster's Coach, during an interview he conducted with me for the Work Utopia Podcast. I was pleased to do it, as Alexander asked me questions with great enthusiasm, excitement, and high energy. I understood that he was in the process of life transformation, and could not refuse tagging along!

I could never forget Alexander, simply because of the first question he posed to me: "What do I identify with more, thunder or lightning?" Of course, I picked both! It was a unique and dazzling way to start the podcast!

Alexander conducted a fabulous interview, and he managed to extract a great deal of information from me, in a very short period of time. I could have earned thousands of dollars in coaching fees with the content that I shared, but I gladly answered his questions, and gave as much as I could to his listeners. I recall being so impressed after the phone interview, I immediately called him back to thank him for having me on his program. It was a wonderful experience and well worth my time.

During our time together, Alexander was in a metamorphosis, utilizing the goal-setting system that I had taught him. He told me that he had finally decided to do the things that he loved, and the dividends for him immediately became life satisfaction, excitement, and happiness in every area of his life. Now, he offers this book to show you how to successfully achieve the same - through the execution and creation of a podcast. Amazing!

In 2017 alone, Alexander created and produced nearly 200 podcast episodes! He is a trained Certified Professional Life Coach, with membership and recognition from the International Coaches Federation, and he is the world's first authentic Certified Podcaster's Coach. He has a great amount of experience and wisdom. He has struggled, survived, flourished, and then thrived. If you want to transform, follow in Alexander's footsteps.

Read this book and feel blessed that you are a podcaster. If you are not one yet, get on it! Do it for fun or business. Follow Alexander Laurin, the Podcaster's Coach, and get inspired and grateful for the amazing, successful, podcasting journey that lies ahead of you.

Raymond Aaron
New York Times Bestselling Author

Foreword
By Gary Leland

I first spoke to Alexander Laurin in September 2017. I was a featured guest on his program, The Podcaster's Life. Both of us were Presenting on September 31st for the annual International Podcast Day Celebration. Alexander presented several hours before I co-presented with my good friend, John Lee Dumas.

I enjoyed my time with Alexander and understood what he was trying to do - help other Podcasters. I understood that what mattered most to him was getting the best information out of his guests, so that his listeners (who are also podcasters) could improve their podcast. I remember giving some advice on starting a podcast and later monetizing one.

I began a new business and podcast, 'The Crypto Cousins Podcast', and Alexander, once again, dug into my process, giving me the opportunity to help others through what I already knew. In addition to podcasting, we also have 'giving to others' and 'helping others succeed', in common.

What impressed me the most, during our second interview, was the evolution of Alexander's show. Since our last talk, he introduced a 'Podcaster's Nerd Out Challenge' & 'Micro Podcast Improv' portion to his show. I had a great time. I have been podcasting since 2004, and this was the first time that I attempted a comedy improvisation on a podcast. It was very fun.

I am pleased to share this with you in this foreword about Alexander Laurin, The Podcaster's Coach. Through his podcast, and this book, he has become a credit and valuable resource for our podcasting community.

Gary Leland
Academy of Podcaster's Hall of Fame Member, Podcast Movement Co-Founder, and Host of The Crypto Cousins Podcast.
GaryLeland.com

Introduction

Being Who You Want to Be—Right Away!

I will share my story and example of becoming what I wanted to become: a successful person. I accomplished this with the help of a podcast, and the process of podcasting. I know what I didn't want: to remain in the business world of recruiting and staffing. I have infinite passion for podcasting. I have grown by leaps and bounds, and podcasting was the tool that helped me evolve quickly, in a short amount of time. I wanted to start a business around podcasting, help others, and show the potential of what they (people), and it (podcast), could do together.

I was finishing my International Coaches Federation's approved coaching program, and the instructor was talking about niches one evening. He gave numerous examples, and one stuck out the most: speaker's coach. I thought to myself, "What about a Podcaster's Coach?" I was loaded with instant excitement. I would apply my skills as a Life Coach, and focus my practice on the podcaster.

After class, I went online to search for *Podcaster Coaches*. I found *Podcast Coaches*, but they all offered a more consultative approach, like technical or performance services. I could not find anyone with ICF (International Coaching Federation) recognition, nor life coaching, and I thought that I could actually become the very first to market. Http://www.podcasterscoach.com was available, so I snagged it, and just like that, I became the very first, true to the coaching profession, Podcaster's Coach. And I had my new coaching business, just like that.

This filled me up with fear too. There have been people podcasting since the early 2000s. I started in 2017. Who did I think I was?! Impostor syndrome crept itself in for a while; however, I had momentum on my side. I was undergoing life transformation with the help of my podcast, and I had a new mantra in mind that I could finally decide to practice. It went like this: only do what you love, and the money will follow.

I became the Podcaster's Coach, and I had the property to prove it: the URL, and every social media handle that says podcasterscoach. Should the social media universe challenge me, or try to take me down, then I would approach all of it with compassion—for them, and myself. I had to give myself a chance.

So, I began. I knew that people would not be listening to me anyway. It would take time to build a following, and a regular listenership. The only pressure that existed was the pressure that I had put on myself. That was completely my choice.

In terms of podcasting wisdom, I was overflowing with it, and it has formed the foundation of this book. In terms of actual episodes and experience, I had just over 100 episodes produced before becoming the Podcaster's Coach. I knew the best way to learn was through others, so I began to interview podcasters, on my podcast. They would call that a *meta-podcast*—a podcast about podcasts. Meta-podcast somewhat described my show, but I was mostly interested in the people behind the podcasts. I wanted to understand them better. I wanted to know if they had learned all of the things that I did, and what more they had learned.

All of my guests have been my teachers. They have confirmed most of what I knew, and they taught me a great deal about technical things, monetization strategies, branding, and business development. They've also entertained me a great deal with their podcasts. I have listened to them all, and have listened to so much creativity. I do consider all of this to be art, so when I listen to a new podcast, it's as if I am attending their exhibit. I can listen to their style, their choice of music, their timing, their emotions, and of course, their message. Long ago, I lived in Ottawa, Canada, and I had countless art galleries at my disposal. I attended them regularly. After I moved, I lamented on what I left behind, and had easy access to. In a way, I have modern art at my disposal, easily consuming podcasts as it fits my schedule, and I rarely look back on what I used to have.

That's how I wanted to become, and then became the Podcaster's Coach—just like that! I have heard it before: if you wish to become something, start by being it, and as you go, you learn to become better at it. Starting a podcast might be the easiest way to start being the person you want to be.

Podcasting for Self-Transformation

This is a book about personal success, and living a happy life. It is not a technical book that will guide you step by step in podcast production, nor will it provide you advice on getting rich.

In terms of advice on starting a podcast on your own, I will offer you what almost every other Podcaster will offer you: just do it.

Many people get overwhelmed with technology, very easily. It doesn't have to be that way for you, if you cannot get started. You have all of the tools at your disposal to create a podcast—with no initial investment.

Podcasters who tell you to *just do it* will also tell you that your first few podcast episodes will not be very good. It is like that for most of us. It was like that for most of the great podcasters. Go back and listen to your favorite podcaster's first episode, and hear the difference.

From their first episode to present day, they have grown immensely. Their show, and skills, have drastically improved, and they have learned a great deal about podcasting...and themselves.

I started off with a cheap computer head set that I had for about 5 or 6 years. My co-host didn't even have an external microphone. He simply spoke into a laptop mic. It was fine. We were complete amateurs. After about 3 or 4 episodes in, the sound quality started to irritate me, so I began looking into a microphone. While I looked, we continued on. The show was evolving and changing quickly. We were very excited about it.

Yes, they were absolutely awful. On a scale of 1–10, they were all a 1. Nine months later, I am much better, and still learning all the time. In another year, I will be even better.

You can do this for free. You can start right away. If you have not started, it's time you took your first step on your podcasting path. Google *free* and *podcasting*, and you will find a few options. Get an account, record an audio file on your phone, and then upload it. Worry about the rest later. No one will be listening to you anyway (as you start).

Practice, plan, and evolve. You can work on the show as you go. If this is your passion project, just do it and have fun.

If this is a compliment for your business, you won't start out amazing, but you might find help and support to get going quickly. As a bonus for purchasing this book, if you want to make a small investment on getting your podcast started (for your business, or as a fun tool to use to help you achieve more success), please visit www.TheBook OnPodcasting.com for a significant discount code on the *Startup Podcast Program* that I offer. My clients become members of the *Business Podcast Network*, which includes Podcaster Masterminds for our collaborative podcast community.

I have created multiple podcasts. When I began *The Podcaster's Life*, I had accumulated enough experience and expertise that I could confidently use my content as a marketing piece for my business. I went through this amazing journey with my first 3 podcast series, and this book is a reflection of what I have learned about podcasting, and the power of it as a tool for transformation, personal growth, and different areas of life that offer feelings of success.

So, don't wait. Execute your idea. Consider it practice if you have to.

When you start, your life will improve, and you will feel like you are doing something worthwhile with your time. This book will share many ideas on recording success through your podcast. Hold on to any one, and live well. Nothing is perfect, but the process of podcasting, and being creative, will constantly get you striving toward self-actualization—if you set this as your intention. I always say, "If you want to have a great podcast, have a great life first." You can use podcasting as the tool to take you to that great life.

Podcast 101

This incredibly short section is for those who are interested in the podcasting world, and perhaps this book acts like an introduction. In the past, I would hear the term *podcast* and not fully understand it, but found it interesting and something that I would like to explore. To be honest, when I first heard the word, I felt something deep inside me that I couldn't comprehend. It was as if podcasting was calling out to me. As strange as this might sound, I can reflect on that initial feeling from the word *podcast* today, and understand; I have built a life and profession around the podcast genre. If the word calls out to you, and you purchased this book, then you must start a podcast. Podcasting has the ability to greatly enhance your life.

So, if you are new, what is a podcast?

A podcast is a series of audio files hosted on the internet. They are stored on a website's database and server, and are accessible on-demand. They are free and can be consumed from a variety of desktop websites or podcast apps, like Apple Podcasts or Google Play. There are a large amount of podcast players available for free, or for a small fee. Simply search for *podcast player* in the store of your mobile phone, or tablet, and see all of the available options. Once you have a podcast player installed on your phone, start you podcast journey by doing a keyword search, and find some amazing podcasts to listen to. You might not like many, but you may love some.

From there, you will have the option to *subscribe* to a podcast. This will give you access to every published episode, to the particular podcast that you subscribed to. The shows are in order of date, newest to oldest. Your podcast player has settings that you can change to suit your desire on how you wish to receive the podcast.

When you start, you will see that podcasts will range in duration and frequency. There are no rules. Podcasts can be daily, weekly, or monthly, and they can be as short as 5 minutes, or as long as 2 hours. You will eventually determine what your podcast appetite will be. I suspect that you will listen to many podcasts in the beginning, but you will eventually find that happy medium of how much time you can spend to listen, and the variety that suits your lifestyle.

There are many types of podcasts, and the list grows every day. You can find shows in just about any genre: business, finance, marketing, science, technology, people, mystery, true crime, podcasts about movies and TV, sports, motivation, news, and current events, etc....

Podcasts change personal and professional lives. The podcast community is warm, inviting, and inclusive. Greetings, and welcome into the world of podcasts!

Chapter 1
My Journey Toward Success

"Life is just a journey." – Princess Diana

The Day and Moment Things Changed

I was lying on the couch. I was sprawled, the kids were not in the room wanting to play with me, and I was watching some mindless television show. A few months had passed since a very painful soccer injury, and I was just beginning to become mobile again. The doctor thought that I might have torn my pectoral muscle while diving for a ball. It was harsh, daily pain. I stopped all physical activity and went back into my old eating and drinking patterns. It was an exhausting existence, and I felt depleted.

Suddenly, my wife Kim ran into the room, bursting with happiness. "I got my ticket!" she proclaimed. "I am going to see Tony Robbins live! I can't believe this! Only $75. I am so happy!" I congratulated her, but I did not understand, nor comprehend this level of excitement. I don't think I have ever seen my wife with this level of excitement before.

After she left, I laid there and reflected on my body—my belly, my overall posture, and my pain—and then, my mind: my boredom and my dissatisfaction with my current situation. My wife had left the room, but the residue of her excitement remained in the spot where she had stood. I suddenly decided to act completely out of character. "Hon, can you get me a ticket too?" I hollered from the couch. "Really?" she yelled back.

"Sure, I'll go with you. "We'll find someone to watch the kids, and we'll go together." She bought the ticket, and we had a date together.

I later found out that she found a deal to become VIPs for the upcoming Wealth Expo, in Toronto, which featured Tony Robbins. I knew who he was, but I had never heard him speak. I was not that kind of guy. Never did I show any interest in motivational speakers. I listened to some speakers when I was in need of motivation to make cold calls for my business, but these speeches came in short doses. The wealth expo seemed interesting when I looked at the itinerary, but I didn't know anyone, except for Tony and Jim Treliving. I thought, if anything, $75 was worth seeing Jim speak live in person.

Oftentimes, in the past, I backed away from my wife's enthusiasm. During our marriage, she became very *holistic,* and dedicated her time and energy into healthy living. She is an entrepreneur, an amazing Podcast Editor, and a Certified Holistic Health Coach. She has never swayed from her interest in optimal living and personal growth. Name any great speaker, and she seems to have some knowledge of him or her. She is a vehicle of positivity. She has mentioned that I have, at times, been her greatest teacher, as I was very difficult to live with! She is a wonderful person and a committed mother, and marrying her was the best decision that I have ever made.

As the days passed, her excitement about the event never diminished. I faked it often, smiling and trying to express some excitement, but I was challenged to convince myself fully. I recall telling myself to let go of my identity that I was grasping onto. Despite all of my hard core Buddhist lessons, I was not practicing fully. I knew I was holding on to these ideas on who I thought I was: serious, shy, reserved, and dismissive (to name a few). This was my best chance to practice letting go—letting go of Alexander Laurin—and ridding myself of the past understandings that I had of myself...and start having some fun! This was my ultimate goal.

When the day finally arrived, we began our date. There was a whole host of seminars to attend, and we planned on doing things separately, but we ultimately stayed together the whole time. The place was jammed packed. The host tried to get the crowd cheering and excited to learn about wealth. Kim, and most people, were on board, but not I. I was still holding on. I kept having this inner dialogue about it. I looked at my wife and told myself that I better not ruin this for her, and I had to somehow match her energy. I commenced with a greater effort.

Kim was ultimately there for Tony Robbins, and no one else. I was letting go and really enjoying being with my wife. We sat for hours (which was a great idea because 10,000 people wanted to be as close as possible) until this gentleman, named Raymond Aaron, came up on stage. I had never heard of Raymond Aaron before, but he was immediately awesome. He was a great speaker who had me captivated right away. He was an older fellow, 72 years of age, but he had tremendous energy. He proceeded to talk about all of his accomplishments. It sounded like he completely turned his life around at 36 years of age, became goal orientated, and never looked back. He created his own system called Monthly Mentor® Goal Achievement Program; one-by-one, he listed all of the goals he accomplished. He did things, while older than me, that I never imagined that I could do. When he was 60, he participated in, potentially, the world's toughest race: a one-month, 350-mile foot race to the North Pole, called Polar Race. This man was truly amazing, and he said all of the right things to me. He offered a mentorship program, and he lived in Toronto, and I thought that this was almost too good to be true. Sure enough, Kim signed us both up.

When Kim arrived back at our seats, she was overjoyed. While she was away, signing us up, the people in front of me were completely bashing Raymond. They were calling the whole presentation a joke, and that people were total suckers for buying in. Part of me wanted to believe them, but I fought this hard to keep my energy up. *Side note: these people were foolish, as his program has helped me a great deal. It just goes to show you that you really have to work hard to not allow people's negativity to penetrate your happiness and desires.*

When Tony Robbins finally arrived, 10,000 people went totally nuts. I was rather shocked when everyone around me was screaming and jumping, and going completely bananas. I thought to myself, what the hell did I get myself into? I've been to crazy concerts where people were excited to watch a band, but this was a concert on steroids. Kim was going crazy with excitement, so I decided to try to go crazy too. Tony Robbins promoted energy, and he instructed us to scream and jump, and go nuts. He wanted to teach, and he didn't want it to be in the way that we normally learn—while sitting. He really wanted us to jump. I finally did it. I completely let go of my identity. I became the spirit with energy, joining the other spirits in the joyful frenzy. Next to me was a fellow who seemed very surprised but fully engaged. The fellow he was with mimicked who I thought I was: unwilling to participate, eyes rolling, no energy, and I suspect, really wanting to leave the convention center. Tony Robbins was an excellent teacher who served as a reminder to stick with my goal of letting go.

Tony presented for over 3 hours, and it was fascinating as to how long the energy momentum continued on. He could have kept going on and on, and the audience could have kept jumping and screaming, but alas, it came to an end. We had the best time, and better yet, we had the best time together. I am so incredibly grateful to my wife.

This one day, and night, created a brand new start.

I had new teachers and mentors for areas of my life that needed help. I started my new podcast—The Work Utopia Podcast—right away, and I published daily.

I fully absorbed Raymond Aaron's Monthly Mentor® Goal Achievement Program, and I finally found a goal setting system that made a huge difference. I was creating goals for different areas of my life, and I was achieving them; at times, I was over-exceeding. Time seems to fly, and a month can really pass us by quickly, but on the first day of the month, I start with new goals, and by the end of the month,

I have my results. Unconsciously, as the days began and ended, I was on my way and making progress—measurable progress. Today, I am focused, healthy, and brimming with purpose.

From that time till now, I have learned so much about life, success, and the wonderful digital medium of podcasting. I will share with you what I now know, and hope that you can relate, learn, and reflect on the words in this book.

Listening to podcasts have changed me. Podcasting, the process and tool, has helped me transform.

My Rocky Path Toward Success

I have set myself up for success. You can too. I took a hard, bumpy path. You don't have to.

My life became easier and happier when I expanded the definition of success. I used to believe that success only meant monetary income and material wealth, but I have since changed the definition. Income and wealth are a part of the meaning but not the whole. Success is a cumulative list, with each line item ranked in importance. At the time of this writing, the meaning of success, and the list that formulates its meaning, is dynamic and not static. At the very top of this list, I place happy life, great father, and purpose.

I already had achieved what I thought was success. I have accomplished everything that I set out to do. Life had told me that I should get married, have a family, make a lot of money, and buy a house. In 2005, I stumbled into a career as a head hunter, aka recruiter. I started making an entry level salary as an employee and, within 3 years, I was self-employed and making a six figure income. I completely over-achieved, as I never imagined that I would ever make more than $50k in a year, but I was accomplishing 6 figures, year after year: one year, I am making $12 an hour; the next year, a small salary;

and a few years later, a six figure income. I was incredibly blessed and lucky that I was hired by that recruitment firm that recognized my potential.

Then, of course, it was time for my wife, Kim, and I to raise and build a family. I never drove a car in my life, but I now had the money to buy a car, so I did. At 35, I managed to get my driver's license. Then, I bought my first home. How incredible it was: in less than 10 years, I had achieved total success. Despite all of my previous dumb choices, and my lack of focus, I had made it, and accomplished everything that I thought that I was supposed to. I did what I was told to do: get married, have kids, buy lots of stuff, and get a house.

Once I hit that point, I was in maintenance mode: maintain what I have, live my life, and wait. Wait for what? I didn't know, at the time, what I was waiting for, so I just went through the motions. I was improved, was I not? After all, I had these labels attached to my name: father, husband, and homeowner. It had the opposite effect. I was not improved but rather burdened. Absolutely, I was blessed to have a wonderful wife who would stick with me through good and bad; and, of course, I had these curious and wonderful children, but I was burdened with the weight of maintaining *success* when I was bored of waiting for the motions of life to pass. I lost my vigor. I had already achieved what I was supposed to achieve.

My achievements were big for someone like me. All of my early careers were disasters. I gave up on a business career in my early twenties and started writing poetry for almost 10 years. During that time, I waited tables and had some customer service roles. I was extremely far removed from having a wife, kids, and a home. No banking institution would have ever lent me the money to buy a home during that period.

I will never forget the day when I realized that I was in maintenance mode. I was mowing my lawn. I mow, I think, and I day dream. I lived in a neighborhood where everyone manicured their lawn, and here I was, the business man and former poet, cutting grass. This was my life? This is what I had to do? I absolutely hated mowing the lawn. Here I was, the big shot—the *successful* guy—pushing a lawn-mower, and killing any little insect in my path. What the hell was I doing? I was waiting for life to pass by as I mowed my lawn. I had over-achieved, and this was my reward? My life had become mowing the lawn.

I had struggled with depression on and off for most of my adult life, but the next phase after success— mowing the lawn—had a profound effect on me. I was not a happy person. Prior to this, I was happy sometimes but mostly serious, annoyed by other people often, and up and down depressed. After hitting my peak of success, I became very depressed and no longer made six figures. I hated my line of work as a recruiter. I would acknowledge that the industry was very good to me, but it spat on me regularly. I was losing my desire to pick up the phone and connect people together. Each year, my income would decrease. My son, Remy, was diagnosed with autism; during this time, I was obsessed with trying to recover him from his Autism. He was not born this way, so Kim and I tried to somehow reverse it. I did everything I could, and I paid for anything that I could find that would help, and my income decreased while my debt went up. It was a horrible time, as I was not prepared for my child to be this way. We went on for over a year without a diagnosis because people around us kept telling us that he was delayed. Our home was total chaos, and I was depressed, inadequate, unhealthy, and miserable.

Our second child, Sophia, was born before Remy was diagnosed. Remy is 18 months older. As we dealt with living, and trying to understand and cure autism, we also had another small child to care for. I think the only thing that kept me going was the love that we all had for one another. In between misery, I would love as much as I could. Children will love you no matter what, and my kids are amazing.

But, I carried on—sick. I blamed my wife for everything. Not myself—her! I blamed society for putting me in this position. I began contemplating leaving my family. After all, my cousin did it, and my uncle did it too. Just leave, and start over again. I began hating myself for even entertaining these ideas. I drank alcohol with regularity. I medicated myself with alcohol, and I would do my best to retreat from life. I would hide, drink, and become unavailable. Then, I would be sick the next day. I was often hung over and cranky.

The love from my children really kept me alive inside.

If any of this sounds familiar, or if you can relate in any way, you are fully capable of getting out of any mental funk that you might currently be in. If you have picked up this book, then the love of podcasts are within you. When you launch your podcast, your life will change—believe me.

Throughout my podcasting journey, I have noticed and absorbed many different ways that creating a podcast has changed my life, and the lives of other podcasters. These pages will show you the amazing power of the podcast that is available to you right now. What's most wonderful of all is that it's accessible to all who have access to any kind of microphone. If you do, you can join the community of fellow podcasters, for free. The podcasting world is remarkable and has almost no barrier to entry. It's absolutely amazing!

How One Podcast Episode Saved My Life

I was impacted by a podcast in a very big way.

It may have been in 2012, when a podcast helped me with a great mind shift. At the time, I was suffering badly from depression. I was depressed for many years, off and on. I was really struggling with my business, and I was having no success for months at a time. I had been an executive recruiter— solopreneur—since 2005. I was naturally a good recruiter, so much so that after one year working for a recruiting firm, I knew that I would be successful at my own business, which turned out to be true. My enjoyment of recruiting, over the years, waned for a number of reasons: isolation, rejection, more losses than wins, deceit from both my candidates and clients, and my inability to take care of myself. During the good times, I tried to expand my business, but this was largely unsuccessful as I tried to do everything on my own, with a very limited business acumen.

Since my income was high, I supported my family financially. My wife stayed home and raised our young children. As my income decreased, the expenses never decreased. There were many days when I went to my office and drank beer to escape myself and the situation that I created.

When the fall of 2012 came, I was in my miserable state. My business was a disaster, and I was struggling to pick up new clients. My heart wasn't fully into it, and I could never build up any momentum because the discouragement often resulted in a walk to the beer store. When I didn't drink, I would simply leave early and take long walks.

I had a Blackberry phone at the time, and I would use it while listening to music as I strolled through my town. I discovered Blackberry Podcasts and sought out free content to consume, as my music mix became tiring. I came across a podcast from a Tibetan Buddhist Monk named Lama Marut. I had little knowledge of Buddhism but was drawn to the speaker. As I explored all of the published episodes, one in particular caught my eye: **The Real Cause to Ending Depression (listen here: http://podcasterscoach.com/marut).** The timing couldn't have been any better.

In the most simplistic way that I can put it, if you want to get rid of your depression, instead of thinking about yourself, think about other people. Depression may be caused by the fact that the mind is attached to our individual problems and inadequacies. The topic running in my mind, at all times, was about me. The focus was on all of the negative aspects of my life: I kept telling myself how much I disliked my work; I kept telling myself that I was doing everything wrong; I kept telling myself that I was making mistakes by skipping work and self-medicating with alcohol; I kept telling myself that my home life was too hard; I kept telling myself that my wife did not understand me. On and on this went.

In my case, all of this was amplified by alcohol, poor diet, sitting, and not enough exercise. This became a horrible cycle, and looking back now, it is no wonder why I was in such a dark state. I remember that, one day, I packed up all of my things and moved my office back home, without giving any notice to my landlord. I could not take the additional pressure of another large expense. When I called him, he showed great compassion and allowed me to pay the final month once I closed another deal, which I thankfully did.

When I heard this episode of the *Lama Marut Podcast*, I knew right away that what he was saying was happening with me. My mind was focused only on myself. I started to pay attention to my thoughts and my inner dialogue, and it completely amazed me that I was previously oblivious to my self-talk. It sounded like, if I wanted to end my depression, I had to replace the thoughts of myself with thoughts about another person.

I took a good look at myself and realized that I was wasting my life. I had been going on for months about my purpose in life revolving around mowing the lawn. Embracing that idea was not serving me whatsoever, and I was going down a dark path. I had a home; I had a wife who was always supportive, and beautiful children. They needed me to be at my best, not my worst. I had to start helping myself, and change my focus and perspective.

With Lama Marut's advice, I started to watch my thoughts, catch them, and then insert others. This began with great difficulty, but it was a start. I could hardly keep up with every negative thought that passed, but some I caught and replaced. When a thought appeared about my bad self, I immediately thought about the people in my family that loved me. Once I began this form of mind training, I was on the right path to having a healthier and less depressed mind. It really was exercise. If you want to develop your body, you exercise regularly. In time, you become fit. The exercises, which were once challenging, are not as difficult as before. These same principles apply to the mind. I had to begin to develop the mind muscle that catches the thoughts. It became easier, over time, as I did my best to keep intention present.

It's amazing to think that one podcast episode made such a positive impact on my life.

Lama Marut's advice worked so well that I listened to him as much as I could. For the next two years, I devoted much of my time toward learning and practicing Buddhism. I learned many new ideas, and my world view completely changed. This fed my purpose a great deal. It was no longer about mowing the lawn and maintaining my property; it was about selflessness and helping others. Life became easier when I started to look at the world through Buddhist lenses. Things make more sense to me, and through the dark times of humanity, I have some understanding why things are the way they are, and I am not left with ongoing despair.

As I would no longer label myself a *Buddhist*, nor communicate much with the community that I was once a part of, I still hold this worldview, and it still plays a role in how I interact with others. Karma is always present with me. What you put out in the world (actions and thoughts) will come back to you—bigger. If I continue to have good intentions and kindness, and try to help others, it will always come back and help me maintain this blessed life that I am living.

It really is amazing. One podcast episode helped me change and improve my life, and started me on a path toward helping myself, my family, and fellow podcasters.

How NOT to Measure Success

I think it is a great idea to find a mentor if you are not feeling satisfied, and you are looking for some rocket fuel to move forward with your podcast. I began the *Work Utopia Podcast*, and hired a podcast consultant. Doing so planted many new and exciting ideas. The mentor's focus was podcast income, and his story/background was fascinating. He communicated a potential—very possible and very realistic. I started adopting his advice as my goals.

I was told that if I kept publishing regularly and consistently, I would get on the *New & Noteworthy* section on iTunes, and I should achieve 50,000 downloads in 90 days. Once I do that, then I am well equipped with the stats that will get me sponsors. I was even given a script that I could use to call sponsors. I was really *drinking the cool-aid*.

90 wonderful days pass, and I had 7000 downloads—43000 shy of what I *should* be getting, and I was not on the *New & Noteworthy* section. I felt like a failure, and a terrible Podcaster; my confidence was shot, and I was suddenly extremely unhappy. Did I get hustled and ripped off? Podcasting became negative.

It amazed me how I could love podcasting so much, and then, all of a sudden, dislike the entire process. I took a short break and reflected a great deal about this experience.

I loved checking my stats every day. I was amazed that people were listening to my show, from all around the world. I found great joy. My life was positive, every day, as my topics often reflected self-improvement and motivation. I always thought that I was doing something worthwhile. I had fans. I received compliments. My life improved; but one day, I hated podcasting? It made no sense.

I had a very narrow definition of success: money.

My definition of success actually expanded when I started podcasting. I just didn't realize it, yet. While I consciously focused on money for happiness, I unconsciously focused on things like legacy, accomplishment, relationships, and self-improvement for happiness. I had achieved a high amount of success in many different ways, and it was where I was not successful that my mind decided to cling to. When I realized this, I brought all of my successes to the surface, and I was back on track with my podcast career.

I had followed the wrong advice, and I chose the wrong goal. This was not a SMART goal; it was not realistic.

Don't get me wrong; mentorship is very important, and we need teachers. Be careful with who you decide to hire. The person I hired had been podcasting much longer than most. Perhaps I was getting what was taught from him in 2008? In the podcasting world, 2008 and 2017 are very different times.

Ultimately, this turned out positive. Even through failure, I learned a great deal.

It's very good to be strategic and create goals around your podcast. If you are doing it for business, then learn from those who have built a business with their podcast. It's advised that you have a business plan when you start a business. Don't do what I did. I had no business plan. I just had a dream, and a consultant whispering dreams in my ear.

This book will share all of the ways you can be successful with a podcast. It's not all about money. We live in a day and age where depression is rampant. It's an instant gratification era where many seek satisfaction through social media likes and responses. The middle class continues to shrink, and everything continues to get more expensive.

Podcasting is a huge relief. It's a process that can help you, and it can make your life incredible. It's a medium that also brings people together. It's art. It's a business. It's a passion. It's fun. It's simply amazing and inspiring.

You never have to be stuck with your podcast, except if you focus alone on one area of success: making money. Wealth is a great goal, and I present on the value of business podcast to groups, but allow me to open the door to you about all of the other ways where you can achieve great success. Keep these ideas present in your mind, and bring them to light during the frustrating times when you don't see your listenership grow, or your revenue increase. You might already be experiencing success. You just might not have recognized it.

My goal is to plant the awareness within you that you might be enjoying podcast success—and not even know it! Keep reading, and let me show you how you can bring a new assortment of focus into your life, through your podcast, which has the potential to transform you. My podcasting story is here for you. I have evolved and excelled at a rapid pace in one year alone—so much so, that I have written this book! You can absolutely and positively do the same. Reader or podcaster—embrace all the forms of success available, now.

Chapter 2
Learn, Change, and Have Fun

"The truth is that we can learn to condition our minds, bodies, and emotions to link pain or pleasure to whatever we choose. By changing what we link pain and pleasure to, we will instantly change our behaviors." – Tony Robbins

The school of podcasting offers its students effective and entertaining teachers, and also allows the students ample opportunities to present in front of classes, without creative restrictions. For a student to get the most out of the experience, they must balance and adjust the work that they put into the school.

In a funny way, I see podcasting like this: it's a chance to learn, grow, and have fun, in a measured sort of way. Let me explain...

Learning New Things About Yourself

I always ask podcasters if they have learned something about themselves since they started their podcast. 99% do. A few have said this to me:

"I learned that I don't really feel the pressure to hold back a lot, and sometimes my friends will be like (after the recording is done), "You want to cut that out?" I'm like, "Nah, I don't care man. I'm not going to apologize for who I am."

* * *

"I thought, going into this, there was always that thing in the back of my mind, and in the beginning of "Oh, I'll make a podcast, and it will get popular, and I'll get famous, and like, all the stuff will happen." The more I do it, the more I feel like, "I don't care about that." The fame doesn't matter to me. Whether I'm known doesn't matter to me. If I have ten listeners or ten thousand, I'm okay with that."

"I always thought that I was a good interviewer and listener, but I think I really learned that by doing the podcast."

I have not completely understood what it is about podcasting that teaches us about ourselves (but I am working on it). Perhaps it's our internal dialogue during the process, the voice from within that gets to speak, and our creativity, all pushing the wisdom buttons within. You will most likely learn something new about yourself in your podcast career, too.

I've learned a great deal about *balance*—that abstract word that determines if we are *somewhat content* in the *moment*. Perhaps equilibrium is a better word, but balance is the popular one.

The podcast is my gauge for balance and equilibrium. Everything I do, outside of the podcast, eventually reflects the podcast itself. If I feel overburdened at home, I can tell with my podcast. If my business begins to slow down, I can feel it with my podcast. If I am unhealthy, again, I can tell while podcasting. When I am on top of the world, I produce great shows. I know when I am at my best and when I am not. The process of podcasting works like a tool to prompt reflection on what I should spend some attention to, when I am far from my best.

It might be like that *audible diary* where the podcast is a recording of thoughts and ideas on a time and day. Those feelings are inside myself and embedded in my show. No one is immune from a life's disaster here and there. When I have felt way off balance, I know that I need to take a break at podcasting, and get re-aligned.

Prior to podcasting, I had no real *tool* to really determine this, except perhaps my instincts or behavior at home. I would use a coaching tool called the *Wheel of Life,* on the odd occasion, but not with enough frequency, if I was not employing a coach. I would go with my *gut* or *inner voice*, but I can't recall the countless times that I completely ignored those internal signals. When you are in the podcast, you are living in the moments, and because the podcast is filled with passion, fun, and creativity, it becomes uncomfortable to record with problems or issues looming overhead in the form of a dark cloud. That's just me.

Podcasting is a tool and process for self-development. By simply learning something new about yourself, you grow and evolve as an individual. This is a gift to give yourself, and it can propel you into a better life.

Learning From Others

You can learn about yourself through the process of podcasting. You can learn from others through the process of podcasting. Of course, you can listen to podcasts, but for deeper engagement, you can interview other people and learn directly from them.

When I began my journey as the Podcaster's Coach, I was on a mission to learn as much as I could. I started off my podcast, *The Podcaster's Life,* talking about myself, and sharing the knowledge that I possessed. It occurred to me that if I wanted to share knowledge, it might be easier, and even more enjoyable, to give fellow podcasters another platform to promote, and also provide, *podcasting advice.*

I have successfully acquired an abundance of knowledge from my guests. They have shared so much of what they have done, that I have often tried to duplicate their findings. If I did not have these guests to interview, it would have taken me many years to get to where I am today.

Not only that, but when I need to provide my client's with consultation, I am fully equipped to provide suggestions because I have developed the awareness and knowledge of what is going on within the industry. Some have learned from the top 1% of the industry, and they simply share it on the podcast. I try to make it a point to give my interview guests the opportunity to share the names of those who have mentored them. It's often the likes of John Lee Dumas, Pat Flynn, Daniel J. Lewis, and Cliff Ravenscraft, who have provided the insight and knowledge that has changed the lives of many.

When I began this journey, I realized that I was undertaking a metamorphism; I tried my best to avoid learning from the best of the best. I wanted to learn from my own mistakes, and continue to learn about myself. I have often worried about saying the same things that the top podcast consultants say, but I have come to believe that many people have new ideas at the same time, and it tends to be the ones with the authority and influence that are able to get the word out first. I just happen to be the first *Podcaster's Coach*, but I am sure that others will follow.

As you can learn many things about yourself by executing your podcast, we do need teachers and mentors in life. If you want to learn a new skill, you need someone to teach it to you. If you want to become a better, more successful person, follow the same formula that others have undertaken and are willing to share. Having an interview-themed podcast is the perfect way to do this.

Not everyone will want to be on your show, but some will. If you have someone who knows more than you, and you talk to them about this knowledge, you instantly develop new insights. Additionally, you give others, your listeners, the opportunity to acquire this as well. The more you do this, the more credibility you develop as a host and interviewer; and this reflects more fully on the questions that you ask because you have that new knowledge powered behind all of your words.

There is nothing holding you back from being smarter and wiser. It is as if your podcast is the book, and your guest is the writer. Rather than spend hours upon hours reading a book, you instantly fast track it by getting to the core of insight from the person who answers your questions. It's amazing and powerful, and as I have said before, much easier to do because you have the platform and reason.

"Would you be interested in being on my podcast? I interview thought leaders around the world in the area of personal development."

"Please accept this invitation to become a guest on my podcast. I focus on speaking to the most knowledgeable people in the software industry."

"I have been following your career for quite some time. Would you consider being a guest on my podcast? I interview the brightest minds in finance."

It's really as simple as that. If 10 say no, and one says yes, how will that change you? You will focus on the 1, and they will give you pearls of wisdom; and you will achieve additional ideas that you can begin to implement without painful lessons, and the lack of time."

When It's Time to Change Your Process

If you are unhappy with your podcast, that does not reflect successful recording. There are several things you can do.

I found that I was not immune to the experience of struggling to find satisfaction. At times, like life, the podcasting process may overburden and *cause* a lack of balance. When you excel in certain areas, the others areas may need to catch up. You might be only focusing on your speaking skills, and neglecting the rest, which may not get you the result that you were anticipating. This often leads to stress.

What I found helpful during those times when I felt stressed by the process, was to break down podcasting and divide it up into categories: Editing, Purpose, Content, Planning, Speaking,

Relationships, Financial, and Promotion, eliminating any that I may have wanted to delegate, in order to adjust my schedule.

Examples
- Editing: Your skills level with Audacity; the amount of time being spent on editing.....
- Promotion: Marketing, social media, etc....
- Financial: Podcasting expenses, monetization, budgeting, etc....
- Relationship: Partners, co-hosts, friends, family, etc....
- Purpose: Your mission, your why, your legacy, etc....
- Planning: Time management, scheduling, coordination, etc....
- Speaking: Podcast performance, interviewing skills, etc....
- Content: Creativity, ideas, relevant topics to share, etc....

Here's my personal example, which I am sure many podcasters will be able to relate to: The major part of the show, *The Podcaster's Life*, is based on interviews with other podcasters. At times, when I announce that I am booking guests, the response can be overwhelming—in a positive way but still overwhelming. I have interviewed everyone who agrees to share their time and their life, if I have gone public with interviews openings. There have been some moments where I have been unhappy with this. It felt like too much at times, and I wondered what I was doing wrong to feel this way. You can't escape life's ups and downs, even when it comes to podcasting. But when you recognize when you are down, you pay attention to it, and you lift yourself back up.

In reality, every interview, once complete, was worth the stress. The stress, however, told me that there must be a less discomforting way.

When you are done, it's very important to take a step back, look at everything, and determine what you need to work on. When I looked at all of the categories of my podcasting process, it was clear that I was most unsatisfied with editing. I reflected only on this, and I tried to determine how I could improve and eliminate the stress. I actually did enjoy editing, but only in little doses. What I was doing, at the time, was spending an entire day editing.

Instead of spending most of a work day on editing several interviews, if I used an extra 45 minutes, after the completed interview, to edit, it would eliminate the tediousness of editing hours on end. It worked like a charm.

This took me out of a funk. Another editing funk crept in later. It was the same process: review all of the categories, reflect, and adjust. I've done things like edit as much as I could on a Saturday morning, or only edit an episode the day before a show needs to get published, and even do it LIVE STREAMING, and don't edit it all!

Doing a live streaming episode has become my favorite way to do it. It adds a layer of nervous energy, prior to hitting the *go live* button, which I uncomfortably enjoy. It tells me that I am alive and that I can do anything I want, if I put my mind to it. If I don't go *live,* and I pre-record, I now use the power of delegation, and send my files to http://www.podcasteditservice.com.

If you are out of balance with your program, but perhaps you determine that it's not necessarily your podcast, then it's time to take a big picture overview of your life. Podcasting is a tool toward happiness, growth, fun, and fulfillment, but it is not the *be-all and end-all*. Take a look at all of the other areas of your life, like your health, career or work, financial, personal growth, environment, family and friends, and social, for example. If you improve and work on these areas too, you will have a better podcast. The happier that you are, the more energy that you will have. The more zest you have, the more people will be attracted to you and your voice.

Get into the habit and routine of checking in with yourself. If you need a Podcast Success Coach, reach out to me at http://podcasters coach.com. If podcasting is your number one passion, reflect on all of the categories within the creation and production of your show. If no solution comes, then look outside the podcast. Use your inner wisdom to guide you. Perhaps the voice within you tells you that the podcast is suffering because of relationship issues. Consider that the *spirit* of your podcast is a friend, beckoning you to live well, so that they (your inner life) may also flourish.

When It's Time to Change Your Podcast

Most of the time, your podcast will change naturally. You won't have to force it.

Other times, you will be compelled to make some changes. Change is good. Change is necessary. Change is natural.

I was speaking to an audience on the topic of happiness, coupled with the process of podcasting, and I was full of joy once my presentation was complete. Here, I was having my cake and eating it: presenting and talking about podcasting. It was fun. It had been a while since I had that level of fun. It was more fun than the last batch of my podcast episodes.

Podcasting *is* fun. The peak of it may come sometime at the beginning, when you go solo and deliver a monologue style podcast, and not an interview-based show. Podcaster co-hosts have fun every episode, but when it is you, alone, it's only you and the microphone.

Podcasting can easily turn into work, especially if you are using it as a marketing device. It does not matter if it is for business; the potential of pleasure and enjoyment is forever present.

I loved delivering my speech, and again, it was very fun. When my speech came to a close, it hit me that my podcast, at that point, was not nearly as fun as it could be.

Fun does not exactly come easy to me. Perhaps it's the identity that I held on to as a *serious person*. Perhaps it came from a challenging childhood. Perhaps I didn't know any other ways of having fun, outside of playing sports.

Yet again, the podcast opened up the gateway toward better living. It was time to begin having more fun with my life. It's as though the podcast was a Swiss Army Knife, and I discovered a new utility, or better functionality.

Immediately, I looked at my podcast and asked myself what I could do. I looked and listened to other podcasts for inspiration. I came up with *The Podcaster's Nerd Out Challenge.* This was partly inspired by John Lee Dumas's *Rapid Fire* portion of his *Entrepreneurs on Fire* podcast. I borrowed the *Family Feud's Fast Money Round,* and viola, a 60-second game show was born. Game shows *are* fun.

I thought more of the concept of game shows, fun, and humor, and I came up with the *Micro Podcast Improv,* a 3 to 5-minute comedy improvisation that I could do with the podcaster who I had interviewed. I was no comedian, but I have always loved the fun from that comedic improvisational television program, *Whose Line Is It Anyway?* No one was doing it, so I decided to bring it in.

The results have been outstanding. By introducing fun, it has created greater bonds with my guests. I can interview someone, who I don't know at all, talk to them for 20 minutes, put them through a game show, and then later get them to do improvisational comedy with me. It's great fun, and it brings laughter into my life on a regular basis. That laughter was not there before.

You will know when it's time to change the show. I am wrapping up my season, and I know that season number two will be different. Use podcast seasons as a guide to potential change. Borrow those television ideas, where once the season is over, the next one returns, with new twists and turns. I am seeing other podcasts do this now; or, even wrap the show up and call it a series. Use what worked, and create a new show, if it makes sense. It's a great time to take a break, access your creativity, look back, and rejoice, and make it better for yourself, and your listeners.

Excitement When You Start

The beginning to any podcasting journey is great fun. We all start off as podcast listeners, and we think to ourselves, *I want to do that too!* As I have mentioned, it's accessible to all those who possess any kind of microphone, but the main thing stopping aspiring podcasters is themselves.

When the stars align, and you start, it's exciting. I remember having great anticipation. I researched, planned a little, and set a date. It was becoming more and more real as the days passed and the recording date approached. Those were really good days. You deal with the ups and downs of daily living, but in the back of your mind is the idea that in your future is the identity of a podcaster. We love what we have heard from others, we want a piece of it, and we are going to get it!

I recall sitting in front of my laptop, opening up Skype, triple checking that my recording software was functioning correctly, staring at my notifications, and waiting for my co-host to come online. He showed up on time, we de-briefed, and then we recorded an 18-minute premier podcast episode.

It was nervous fun for me. My co-host was very much at ease and was more of a natural than I was. I was often *thinking* and not fully *listening*, but I knew I was new, and told myself to be at ease. I took it more seriously than I had to; after all, I was wearing an old head set, and recording in my pajamas.

All in all, it went well. The co-host was my cousin, who I spoke with often on the telephone. We basically had a regular conversation, with hockey being the topic. I had podcast fever.

When we were done, I spent some time editing, with the very basic knowledge that I had. I uploaded my .mp3 file to SoundCloud, filled in all of the details, and stared at the publish button for a while. I double check, then triple check, everything. Finally, with a click of the mouse, it was officially a podcast, and I was officially a podcaster.

As funny as it sounds, I was on cloud nine. I felt newly accomplished that I was doing something worthy of my time. It was fun and new; it was something to break the monotony of daily living, and it gave me a special feeling, as podcasts and podcasting were not yet mainstream.

It would be a month before I invested in a microphone. I spent a total of $100 on a microphone, pop filter, and boom arm. When it was all set up, it was further proof that I was a podcaster. Now, I had the set up. I approached my *studio* as if I were a radio broadcaster about to give the world the much needed info that they were looking for.

This was a special time for me, which also provided many lessons. Our podcast lasted 12 episodes, but it did not deter me in the least bit. In retrospect, I would have planned better and chosen a much happier topic. It felt more like a roller coaster as we podcasted on how bad our team was playing. When they won, it was great. When they lost, which they did most of those 12 episodes, it was not as fun as it could be. I realized the potential in podcasting, and how amazing the experience could be if the topic pointed toward happiness, with content representing good and worthiness.

Starting a podcast is an amazing experience. I have coached others into starting, and it is always a huge thrill for the two of us. We have passion within us, and having the opportunity to have the ear of others from around the world is an amazing feeling to have. The non-podcaster cannot say this. Perhaps a blogger or video blogger may feel this way, but there is something special, not to mention easier, about just using your voice to share your story and interests.

If you want a taste of this, you can have it. One of the beautiful things about living is having the opportunity to feel and embrace your uniqueness in a positive way.

Podcasting Has a Formula for Fun with a Co-Host

I had a co-host for a short time. We had a great time recording together. It didn't last, for a few reasons: time commitment, content, and scheduling. We were planning on the fly, and it ultimately did not work out.

I have listened to co-hosts have the best time with each other. It's obvious through the laughter. I, myself, have a great time when the co-hosts are having so much fun.

Podcasting has a formula for fun when there are multiple voices on the show: Passion Topic (which means an interesting topic, which the host loves talking about) + mutual respect + lightheartedness + not taking oneself too seriously = fun. Being on topic, sharing opinions in a safe place, and creating something together, which you can later see, hear, and share, is wonderful.

All you have to do, to have more fun with a friend, is start a podcast together. You will have a blast recording.

There are things that are important to keep in mind before you start a program with your friend or a family member. Podcasting has the ability to damage a relationship if it's not planned at all, and is executed off the seat of your pants.

Duties should be divided.

Someone has to manage the podcast hosting, the show notes, and the editing, as well as oversee the actual recording and the promotion. If one person does it all, it may become a source of stress for that person, especially since they have a partner. There are things that co-hosts must do together, like episode planning, and of course, speaking, but it is best if there are shared responsibilities in place. If your co-host cannot make time, or find someone to delegate their share of work, it has the potential to hurt a friendship. The mind loves to focus on the negative. Once the mind decides to get *annoyed* by the inequality from the distribution of responsibilities, it might snowball into something more than just annoyance.

Both should have a somewhat equal passion in podcasting.

Many of us get the podcast bug and take it quite seriously. It's a passion, a love, a joy, and a hobby, infused with the potential of meaning and purpose. If one co-host feels this way, and the other does not, it may also eventually lead to some hard feelings. I have seen it go two ways: the a co-host develops the bug, and makes the podcast a very high priority; or, a co-host maintains their current state of interest in the podcast, happily contributing as they are but unwilling to invest anymore of themselves—more or less, showing up to speak. Shared passion and enthusiasm are key to long-term success.

It's okay to take a chance. It could be a start to your podcasting journey, but if it creates stress and tension, it is better to walk away before it affects a relationship in a negative way. If you are honest, and say that it's becoming too stressful, and that you have fears about continuing, then either come up with a new agreement with your co-host, or walk away and start another podcast. Luckily, it won't take you very long to determine if you have the right partner. If it's your very first podcast, chalk it up to practice. I am forever grateful to my cousin for starting with me. If not, I might have kept delaying.

There are no rules. You can have a podcast for 12 shows, 2 shows, or 100s of shows. You can walk away anytime if it's not fun or enjoyable. Start one, stop one, start another, stop it, and create another, etc. You are providing your listener with entertainment. If it's not fun for you, it probably won't be fun for the person wearing the ear buds on the other side.

It's worth it. Pick a friend and have some fun together. Record your conversations, and share the enjoyment that you have for one another with the rest of the world. It becomes a meaningful activity if you put out happiness and laughter to counter-act all of the negative things that we hear about in the world. It's also making a positive contribution to our global society through friendship, caring, and conversation.

Everything that I know, I have learned from others. I have understood myself better through listening and reflecting. As much as I have adored the world of podcasts, challenges have arisen. It is absolutely worth modifying and changing our approach to keep climbing all of the different ladders of success that we can find.

The podcast can shine a light on the definition and direction of your life, help you realize how to spend your time well, and get to know yourself better. Next are some thoughts and ideas on how to keep your momentum going.

Chapter 3
Living Well

"Without continual growth and progress, such words as improvement, achievement, and success have no meaning." – Benjamin Franklin

Your podcast can help you organize your priorities, and be your motivation to be living the best life possible. Podcasting is a special experience that can open the door to greater meaning and focus. A successful life is one that has direction.

Bye-Bye Boredom

The seed of depression might come from boredom, especially in our instant gratification society. Day in and day out, we live routinely. Except for the exceptions of the population who engage in high energy activities (like sports for example) and other things that involve excitement, we live a bit.......mundane? Forgive me on generalizing, but I've been this way, and many people that I know, outside of podcasting, have been like this too. Eat, work, try to find time for the things you like, spend time with loved ones or friends, go shopping, clean......these are the regular things. When I have needed a jolt of excitement, I've played soccer. This gets the blood flowing and creates comradery within the members of my team. Other than that, I've been involved with many projects that began as exciting but, eventually, fizzled out to dissatisfaction in time. Education has always been interesting, but who has time to study and take notes? If you study, you want to find like-minded people to share these ideas with. I've gotten into the trap of too much reading, which created too much thinking, which eventually would lead me to dissatisfaction.

Over the years, I have learned several ways to avoid my boredom and depression: spirituality, exercise (which promotes our happy genes), and podcasting.

I am not saying that these things will eliminate clinical or severe depression. However, if life is boring, routine, and monotonous, these ideas and activities will raise your spirit. With podcasting, in particular, I found that once I entered the podcast sphere as a creator, my boredom significantly decreased. Podcasting is a time-consuming process that is worth the effort.

There is something special about pushing that publish button. Depending on the type of show that you produce, it could be a long or short time period until you are able to distribute an episode. Once you do, there is a relief. You have this completed project. If you have published it, then it was worth the effort, as you have seen it through.

If you are a podcaster, think about your life pre-podcast. What were you doing with that time you lost to podcasting? I was doing a lot of mundane things, like watching TV re-runs. For some bizarre reason, I used to watch *Judge Judy* almost five days a week. I certainly don't do that anymore. Come to think of it, I don't even remember what I was doing with any of my pre-podcast time, besides that. I can't recall, because so much of it was insignificant and unworthy of memory. There was a lot of drinking, a lot of TV, and just living, or being, or surviving, or paying bills.

I can look at my published episodes and remember something special about each one. I can estimate that each published podcast is between 1–2 hours of time and effort. I enjoy every bit of it. From what I don't enjoy, I find shortcuts to decrease my time. You can't create a podcast living a boring life, unless you set your intention on creating a boring podcast.

There is no boredom in speaking into a microphone, if you want to create a podcast. Planning requires some happy energy, and hitting that publish button is satisfying, with a tad of nervous satisfaction when you start. Perhaps editing and promotion lack a certain excitement, but the process itself is a worthwhile activity.

Podcasters are not living an ordinary life. Podcasters are engaged in podcast activities that counter mild depression and boredom. If you podcast happily, yet the boredom and depression remain present in the process, it is sign of something bigger—perhaps a negative mind, a psychological predicament, anxiety, or other factors that need attention. Help yourself by seeking help.

Try to remember what you did with your time that you replaced with podcasting. Is podcasting more interesting? Does it offer more motivation? Has it been satisfying? Do you remember a highlight to each episode?

If you have been publishing for a while, and you are bored with your podcasting career, switch things up, and consider that you have already evolved upwards in layers of interest. Being a bored podcaster is a blessing in this case. You've already achieved setting yourself apart from the mundane life. Now you are ready raise the bar to even greater heights of interest. Begin to understand how special you are.

Achievement Versus Meaningless Activities

Achievement is an easy word to understand. It's action oriented. What have you done? What are the things that you have accomplished? Do you have a lot of check marks in your boxes?

Podcasting has been an incredible experience for me. I have gone through a lot of personal development during this time, and the podcast was one of the tools that I used to energize myself and make my life better. And while I was creating and publishing, I KNEW IT. I knew what the process of podcasting was doing for me. I had more excitement about life, my purpose was returning with realignment, and I was motivated.

Coupled with my business mentor's advice on goal setting, I started living a life of achievement. Raymond Aaron provided the system, and all I had to do was work at what I loved: podcasting.

Have you ever asked yourself where the time goes? As a podcaster, you will know exactly where your time is going—you can simply look at your podcast RSS feed. I set a big goal for myself, and I chose to publish 20 new episodes per month. I worked on the show with a big chunk of my day, and I checked off every single box I created. It was actually an exhilarating experience, and where I first developed the inspiration to write this book. When I review the months that have passed, I have the proof that I have been getting things done. It's very satisfying.

If you want to live a life with achievement, there are choices that you must start making. It boils down to a matter of time. What are you spending yours on? Five new published episodes is a very lofty goal. At the time, I was scripting the material and producing a 25-minute podcast. Twenty-five minutes would equate to 2 to 2.5 hours of work, excluding *thinking* time. Two and a half hours is a big chunk of your day, especially if you work full time. Perhaps you have a family, and you don't live alone? It's a big challenge to fulfill that time on a daily basis.

I am not suggesting that you do a daily podcast. Some podcasters do one episode a week, and sometimes one episode every two weeks. I have noticed that those who do, have longer, more elaborate episodes and productions. Some podcasters I know will spend an enormous amount of time on editing alone.

So, where does this time come from?

Most people will make the mistake of stealing their sleep time. We absolutely need an adequate sleep. If we sleep well, then we are refreshed the next day. If we are refreshed for our day, we have a more productive day. The temptation is always to stay up later than you should, but don't do it. Look at some other options.

When you become a podcaster, you will begin to learn about the time commitment needed to produce episodes. At first, it will take longer than you expect, but with time and practice, you will get a more accurate picture of what the average amount of time is required to produce your show. Like anything else, you get better and more efficient with practice.

Once that is figured out, it all comes down to choices. If you stay away from your sleep time, then something from your day will need to disappear. If you require 2 hours of *podcast time*, what will you remove to make space?

At this point, you have the opportunity to replace meaningless tasks with meaningful tasks. Podcasting is a positive, worthwhile experience, and if you take away the items from your life that do not serve you, you instantly start living a better life. Of course, we need to rest. We need to *chill-out*. We need a break.

What I eliminated was hockey. It was a hard choice to implement but a fairly easy decision. I realized that I was spending 10 hours a week watching it on television. When my team won, it was fun. When my team lost, it sucked. Half the time, I was not even enjoying the games.

Essentially, I held onto the identity of *hockey fan* and *podcaster*. I had been a hockey fan since I was a very young boy, and I held onto that every season. But, was I *really* a hockey fan? If you split me open, are you going to find a hockey puck? What exactly am I holding onto and associating with? How does this benefit me? My family? Society? Or my legacy? Would there be a significant negative impact to my life if I stopped watching 3 full hockey games a week? Of course, it has no impact whatsoever.

Could I remember all of the hockey games I watched over time? No. Could I remember something about every podcast that I created? Yes! If I played an old episode for a minute or two, I could recall much about the episode and the circumstances revolving its creation. Hockey and sports definitely have lasting memorable moments, but there is something different when you create your own personal memorable moments.

Imagine taking 5–10 hours a week that do not serve you, and replacing it with something that makes you happy and gets you creative. Doesn't that sound great? Each episode that goes by, you can recount: Episode 1–10, yes, you did that! Episode 11–25, you did that too! Fifty podcast episodes?! You got that done! This is living a life of accomplishment. It's about taking your time to do something worthwhile, and distancing yourself away from the things in life that do not serve you.

How about you? What can you remove?

The Creative Element – Free, Present, and Within

Some podcasters will tell you that podcasting is an art form. Many who say this are already practicing an art form like music or writing. The podcasters who struggle with the *artist* label, I think, prefer to associate the term with a certain type of individual, like a painter or a visual artist. I used to feel the same way, often calling art something that was born from toil, abstract thought, or even pain and suffering.

I spent a little less than 10 years working on poems. I was influenced by Leonard Cohen, Charles Bukowski, and Irving Layton. There were times that I imagined being like them, and in those times, I would feel like a *real* artist. I would project the idea of someone I considered an artist, onto myself. Oftentimes, it was dark and lonely, and I must admit, special.

In almost 10 years, I feel that I created 3 good poems. These poems were charged by my love, inspiration, and soul. There was a certain feeling during these writings, where I felt that something out of the ordinary was transpiring. It was an amazing feeling, which I could only produce on a few occasions. I could never find the right language to adequately describe the profound feelings that I had. This taught me that there is something about us that cannot be described effectively with the English language.

Twenty years later, to the best of my ability, I understood how to describe it in a very simplistic way. Podcasting opened the door and helped guide me.

I stopped all art after I stopped poetry as my primary occupation. I traveled to various parts of the world. I met my wife, traveled a little more, settled down, found a job, started a business, began a family, and purchased a home. Some poems were scattered in between, but nothing really stuck. I didn't feel that I could call myself an artist.

When I began my podcasting career, the label of artist returned to me in a subtle way. There was something going on... a familiar feeling. Not exact, just similar, and milder. "Could I be producing art again?" I asked myself.

When I created shows filled with love, grief, beautiful sentences, and spirituality, I felt amazing doing so. It felt as if I was touching my soul, or my soul was touching me. It was more like a dance. It was like that experience I felt as a poet while constructing good poems. I simply say that it was my soul coming out, playing, or perhaps dancing around me. It's almost like feeling a faint breeze from the soul's activity.

Perhaps I can say this because I have previously experienced it in the past with another art form. I felt a strong creative process permeating throughout me in those days. This feeling, during podcasting, has been milder, but I believe it's the same thing. That opportunity is there— through podcast creation—to feel a part of your soul. Podcasters are artists. I am fully convinced of this.

If you can consider this, and open up the possibility that you may be an artist, what would that do for you? Could you see that you are creating audio digital works of art? Could that make you feel special?

Creative expression is alive in all of us. You have the podcast medium. Most people do not. In a way, I think everyone, without having an *artist* label, expresses their creativity in daily living. It could come from landscaping, speaking, or even decorating, but what we ordinarily do is not enough to recognize that special part of our being.

It's amazing to think about the idea that the podcast community is made up of artists doing something very special with their voice, with some helpful technology. Do you realize that you may be doing something more with your podcast than what you originally thought?

Powered by the essence within, you successfully express, and bring out, a part of you that craves for attention.

A Part of a Spiritual Practice

Spirituality comes in various shapes and sizes, and no matter what your preference is, if you act according to the moral and ethical teachings of your faith, then you are living a good life, with purpose.

I am not going to devote time to those who label themselves with a spiritual or religious title, and don't practice their teachings, but rather on those who have a belief and a faith that guides their hearts and actions.

The Buddhist worldview, and the principles of karma, work well for me. Early on, I adopted them, and now it seems that they are ingrained in me. I don't have to think them into the present; they are almost always there. Most of the world's greatest, ancient traditions have many similarities and shared principles. Explanations might be a little different, but all work as a sort of road map or instruction manual to living a good life.

Call it karma, or charity, or compassion, or giving. Helping others is a foundational piece to a religious or spiritual life. It is also a common theme among podcasters: the desire to help others with their podcast. Most will not call it a spiritual service but will be powered by giving, as one of the purposes of the program.

I learned a while back that spirituality is not limited to a couple of hours on Sunday. It can be adopted and practiced anytime, anywhere. I went through numerous episodes, keeping my intention on helping other people, and giving a living prayer before I started. I did not directly tell my listeners what I was doing, but it was there, surrounding the words and the voice.

I found this a great relief in many ways. First, I felt as though I was using my time meaningfully, trying to help others through my message. Second, I was actually practicing my form of spirituality, keeping it present while podcasting. And third, through karma, I was helping myself, and planting positive seeds in the world.

I have spoken with some podcasters who are fueled by God on their show. Their programs are Christian based, and they work hard for the betterment of their community. I have heard some podcasts where the host will speak of their faith, and I can only assume that it powers them in their journey. I have interviewed others who just find it interesting, and are willing to learn new ways to be a better person. Religion and spirituality offers just that.

If you want to live a spiritual life, you can actually use the podcast as a means to practice one. You don't have to tell a soul, either (pardon the pun). First, you need to pick something, if you have nothing. Go with what you were introduced to as a child—something that perhaps you gave up on as an adult. Or, start looking, and choose a faith or system that resonates the most with you. Pick something that has been around over a thousand years, and consider staying away from anything controversial. This is simply my advice and opinion. Consumerism is the new religion, and it is void of depth and inner substance. I like consumerism, but I won't pray to it. Consumerism will someday end, but it's not likely that faiths like Christianity, Buddhism, or Islam ever will.

The End of Your Life and The Bucket List

One of the major themes of Buddhism, that I was attracted to, was death. There was this message of living every day as if it were your last, along with being prepared for your final moments, to ensure peace and a positive rebirth. I had never heard of preparing for your death, and Buddhism was my first encounter with these ideas. You must do your best because you don't know when and where your last breath will occur. If we live our lives positively and with compassion, chances are, we will not leave this world in a fearful state. I'm going with that idea because I have seen others live the end of their days with no regret, nor clinging to the physical world.

As I started to come out of my spiritual box, I decided that I would explore the topic of death in greater detail. I went on a sabbatical from my business, and decided to work with the dying. The easiest entry into this type of work was through Hospice and Health Care. I jumped into a night time Personal Support Worker program and received a certification from the local school board. Additionally, I enrolled in a Contemplative End of Life Care Program at the Institute of Traditional Medicine, in Toronto. I merged the learning of the two—one physical and the other spiritual.

There were no residential hospices in my area, so I volunteered at the local non-profit agency, giving my time for the day program and one-on-one companionship. I was hired part time at a local health care agency as a palliative support worker. I was quickly in the homes, supporting the dying, along with their families.

The physical aspect never bothered me. I already had support worker experience before receiving any certification, from the experience of loving and caring for my special needs son. I always kept the thought in my mind that you cannot go wrong by helping other people. My work with the dying was a real life education on death.

Very few people that I encountered in this work were prepared for their dying. Many people grasped for continued life. Some showed desperation for treatments that only made them sicker. I was shocked to see many dying people spending their final weeks in front of the television, subjected to violence, commercials, and fluff.

There was no end to the compassion that I felt for everyone not dying well. The system seemed inadequate to me. The health care industry seemed to want to control death with regular visits. Many families took solace in this, and called the nurses and doctors the experts on dying. Families spent a lot of time in panic because they did not understand the dying process. Caregivers had no training, little understanding, and they were generally overwhelmed. These people, however, were simply amazing to be dealing with the situation at hand, with the little that they knew. They showed me how resilient and caring a human being could be. They were all sleep deprived, had little emotional support, and were financially challenged because of the inability to work and care for the dying. I felt so fortunate to walk into their homes and give them a break. The human spirit can move mountains.

The highlight of my work was a very peaceful death, where the gentleman, Robert, was sedated. His granddaughter was there for him, and I was able to give him Reiki while she slept. I was instructed to wake her should I think that his last breath was near, but Robert woke his granddaughter on his own, despite being in a sedated state. She woke, came into the room, and claimed that she heard him calling out to her to come to his side. She sat by his bedside, and then he died. It was an amazing experience.

Many dying people I encountered talked about God when I tried to get them to talk about death and their dying, but they did not come across to me as truly believing in God. They would talk about church and not going for many years. I could see that they did not practice their Christianity, nor have it centered in their mind. Many times, the dying did not want to talk at all about what was happening to them, and it pained me when they tried to ignore their reality.

I stopped doing this work, as I had seen enough. I simply found that people were unprepared, nor did they focus on spiritual tools to make sense of their upcoming departure. The health care industry mostly produced individuals focused on their trade and not the conversations. I wanted to learn, and I did, but I did not belong there.

I have seen common simple people, military leaders, and even executives, all dying from cancer. We are all the same, as this life is finite, no matter how you are labeled by others, or who you think you are. Creating a podcast is certainly not going to save you from death, but it can fill your heart as you live. Many people love to use the words *bucket list* for the things that they want to do before they depart for the mysteries of the afterlife. If you have felt this urge and desire, or even placed *making a podcast* on your bucket list, do it now, as life is very short. Once you do, your podcast will be immediately successful.

Your Digital Legacy

Life is very short. You think that you have an idea on how long it will last for you, but you honestly don't know. Many people don't like the topic of dying. Take full advantage of this gift of life.

I had an extremely brief career in hospice and palliative care. I learned a great deal from a non-traditional school (The Institute of Traditional Medicine), books, families, and the dying, or rather, those *living* with a terminal illness. I've seen a last breath, and I have witnessed every stage of the dying process.

None of us is immune. You can work in the steel mill, or be the CEO of a major conglomerate. It doesn't matter what you do for a living, how much money you have, how much knowledge that you have acquired, nor your status in society. We all die. Every one of us.

My children are young, but I wonder, at times, how long I will have. I create in my mind their future sadness when I am no longer present. I make sadness for myself when I have done this. When I move away from the sadness that I fictitiously imagined, I think about what I can do with the life that I am currently living. What kind of lasting impression can I make?

I can be a role model. I can provide my children with love. I can be a teacher. But what else can I do...for later?

This nagged me for a while, especially as I spent time in the *death trade*. I created a goal to begin a legacy project for myself. Then, as I was creating a podcast episode, I came to the realization that I my legacy project was actually underway—my digital audio recording! My program was turning into a motivational podcast, and I was sharing many details on my life and what I have learned. What I was producing could actually be useful to my children. Perhaps they will have some struggles, seek guidance from their departed dad, and then listen to *The Work Utopia Podcast.* When that idea occurred to me, I tried to keep that intention in the back of my mind, with each episode I created.

That experience and realization was very profound and settling. Since then, I have never lamented about the future life of my kids without their father. Logically, it does not makes sense because I do not yet know which one of us goes to the other side first. When these irrational thoughts come up, they fizzle out because a part of me will be available as long as someone is interested in hearing my voice.

I created a memory box to represent my legacy. I put many items in it, along with some videos, and copies of all my podcasts.

When you do a legacy project, what you are doing is leaving behind a life of achievement. Your podcast is a wonderful achievement, no matter the number of episodes published. A great way to preserve your past is to record your successes, achievements, values, and the things that you found meaningful—like the meaning of being a parent, or a friend, or a family member.

Here are some other things you can add to your own legacy project, in addition to your podcast:

- A web page, and videos
- Letters
- Birthday cards for your grandchildren
- A painting or drawing, and poems
- Stories and lessons you've written about your life
- Something that highlights your spirituality
- A little something about your important relationships
- Objects that mattered to you

Google *legacy project*. There are some resources out there to get you started.

Consider the legacy that you are leaving behind to your loved ones, your community, your society, and the planet, for that matter. What messages do you want to leave behind? Are you living the messages? It's a great reflection exercise.

Consider that your legacy project has been underway the moment you published episode one. Your podcast can come from a passion project, or a podcast content marketing strategy, but you can secretly embed your legacy into it at the same time. You can focus and hold on to the wonderful feelings that you have for other people while you record and speak. Not only does this help you resonate with the podcast listener, but it also touches the people who care for you.

The question is, "Are you already, and perhaps unaware of, creating a digital recording of your legacy?" It's yet another amazing component of the podcasting process.

This chapter focused on many of the elements that will assist in a happy life. Doesn't it all boil down to living a happy life? Let's next touch on the topic of finding happiness in podcasting.

Chapter 4
Happiness

"Happiness is not something ready-made. It comes from your own actions." – Dalai Lama

Happiness is a success, is it not? If someone is rich, and miserable, is that success? Would you prefer the state of happiness, or wealth and misery? If you had one moment to live, you would pick the happy moment.

When we started our family, I noticed that my children seemed to have a natural state of happiness. It made me wonder if a natural state of happiness is present within all of us, just crusted over with responsibilities and the adult difficulties we face in our society. If that is true, we need to peel some of it off.

You Can't Podcast on a Theme That Doesn't Feel Right

I picked up this lesson, twice: you can't podcast on what you don't like doing. If you have managed to convince yourself that you will podcast on something that truly doesn't fit your lifestyle, the process of podcasting will set your mind straight. Let me explain through examples.

My second, two-episode, podcast series, was called the *PSW (Personal Support Worker) Podcast*. I previously mentioned my time working in hospice and palliative care. In order to get into this work, I needed certification to get into the health care industry. I took a part-time Personal Support Worker program, from a local school board, for free, at night, weekly, for nine months. It was a bit long but an easy commitment to make for a couple of hours a week. I didn't learn anything about death and dying but mostly procedures on caring for people in a health care setting. These lifelong skills will come in handy should I ever need to help a loved one, a close friend, or anyone in my circle who would be in need.

I had this idea, since I was no longer in the health care field but had certifications, I could create a new business, and sell coaching services to health care workers. I created an interview-based show: one part, short monologue; one part, PSW interview. It was exciting to create this new type of show, and I learned a great deal, but I ultimately did not want to be in this industry. I got out of it for a reason: I didn't belong. Working with the dying, I found very meaningful at times, but health care was not for me. Despite that, I convinced myself that I could keep my foot in the door by creating a podcast, and building a new business around it. After two episodes, my inner wisdom took over, and I knew that I could not spend any more time on this project.

The second lesson appeared while I was recording *The Work Utopia Podcast*. Once my health care work experiment ended, I restarted my old enterprise software recruiting company, Zencareers. Everything was there—my process, my documentation, my contacts since 2005—and I needed no training, just a dedicated phone line. It was simply a matter of cold calling and getting job orders. It was an amazing contrast: a low, hourly, part-time wage in health care, to $25,000 recruiting commission fees.

It was the same old story—I dialed for dollars—but I was tired and bored of recruiting, despite the big payoffs. The *Work Utopia Podcast* was what I thought work could be. I have heard countless negative stories from employees, and employers, which I often thought were ridiculous, and a waste of life force. If people simply had more respect for one another, and practiced honestly a little better, there would be less misery in the workforce. I started my podcast for two reasons: to promote myself, and seek out great employers to interview, who would then teach other employers how to keep and treat employees.

The first handful of episodes were about recruiting. I loved the process of podcasting, but I did not enjoy talking about recruiting and staffing, despite my level of knowledge. It only became a matter of time that I had to stop what I was doing. I was still making a living with recruiting, but I could not make it a part of my podcast. It became increasingly difficult to talk about with my listeners. In 2014, I received a Life Coaching Certificate, and began offering Career Transition Coaching. This started to take over the podcast because coaching was something that I still enjoyed doing. The next thing you know, my podcast was turning into a daily motivational program. It was at that point, my life began to transform, all through the process of podcasting.

I have listened to many podcasts where the hosts and the guests are talking negatively about a subject—but there must be a layer of pleasure in what they say? I found, in my hockey and health care podcast, that I did a lot of complaining. Recording my complaints was not living a good life, I told myself. The more negativity I put out, the less happy I was. I can only speak for myself, but doesn't it make sense that the more complaining you do, the less satisfied you become?

The truth should come out for you when you are podcasting. If you manage to convince yourself, like I did, on creating a podcast on something that you don't inherently like, the podcasting process will touch your inner wisdom, and prompt you to make a move toward something better. A successful life is one where you do what you love by not ignoring, nor remaining in conflict, with your inner voice. Learning to become more honest with yourself is an important part of living a good life.

Positive Messaging

I had become turned off, for a number of years, by all of the negativity that comes out of the workplace. As I continued to work in this field, I started using the podcast to counteract all of the negativity that entered my mind. I can't recall if it was intentional, but it was dearly needed. I was goal setting, and I had my first business mentor, which added rocket fuel to my podcast and to my life.

Ultimately, you get what you focus on. As I started podcasting on topics that I wanted, I started to get what I spoke about. One episode was about *Eliminating the Negative*. Sure enough, I became more mindful of the negative in my life. Another was about the *Things That Make Us Happy*, with the same result: more mindfulness on moving more toward being happy. And other episode, *Battling Frustration*, helped me think about tools to take it easy, de-stress, and relax more.

Next thing you know, I am talking about spirituality, the positive aspects of entrepreneurship, meditation, patience, dumping negative people, goal setting, habits, writing, caring for others, regret, and being present. Each time, I took my own level of understanding of these topics a notch higher.

Podcasting is a platform to announce all the wonderful gifts of life, to teach others, to learn, and grow. I mentioned earlier that I transformed while podcasting. What helped was to pay attention to the blessing, the lessons, the uniqueness, the talents, the teachers and mentors, and the strength within. This was merged with the excitement to create, produce, and share my voice, in a podcast.

A successful person is a happy person. If you want to become a happier person, or amplify your happiness, you just need to become a podcaster who cares about the subject.

I don't understand the habits of our society. We have newspapers, news radio, and TV news, which focuses on the negative and horrible in the world. These mediums only persist because there are enough eyes and ears willing to invest time in them. Through my experience on recruiting alone, I can say that I have had thousands and thousands of conversations with different people. I would wager that 99% of these people were good and honest. If we accept that number, that leaves 1% of the inhabitants, on this planet, to be bad and dishonest. Yet this becomes the focus for the so-called *media*. I quit paying any attention to this for many years. When it trickles into my life, it's sad, and I become horrified because I am desensitized from much of violence. I choose happy.

Some people think I am a fool to not be *informed* this way. I accept that, and I am good with that. I see the world as a beautiful place, with amazing people. I have a minimum of 20 conversations a month with different podcasters. I only try to focus and remember the wonderful characteristics within each person. Call me crazy.

There is an element of success in being able see the world as a good place. You can take the approach and see the world as another form of Hell, if that works for you. At least be a good person in Hell, make the best of it, and find happiness in a challenging place. Imagine, finding happiness in hell? I am not talking about having mental illness or an unfortunate psychological malady. I am talking about having gratitude in your life, despite the circumstances where you may find yourself. Yet another amazing aspect to this life is that you can actually move closer to gratitude, and grateful living, through a podcast. It's a matter of the content you create and publish.

You can create a podcast on all of the things wrong about life and the world. If you do, that is what you will get. If you create a podcast on the joys of living, the wonderful qualities of people, and the good ways of living, that is what you will get too.

Becoming a New You

If you think about it, you are a *new you* all of the time. Your body is constantly changing. You may not be seeing big changes every day, but there is no denying that you are aging and growing older.

Does the mind change too? Of course! I change my mind often. Some others change it less frequently. I don't know exactly what the mind *is*. There is an idea, which we accept, about the mind being in our heads, but we can't actually see it or locate it anywhere. Depending on your belief system, you might even think that it is located in your heart.

I often refer to my podcaster listeners as *The Listener*. Now, I can refer to you as *The Reader*. It's my identification of you. As I identify you, you identify yourself, and I identify myself.

I identify myself as speaker, author, teacher, podcaster, father, husband, son, and friend. I also identify myself as someone who eats too many french fries, and is a chocolate lover, an impulse shopper, a science fiction fan, etc. There are many layers to the identity that we give ourselves—good, bad, positive, and negative.

I once heard about the concept of clinging to the identity of yourself—the one that holds you back, and never serves you in a meaningful way. If I identify myself as an individual with an *all or nothing* personality, do I not, in a way, re-enforce this? If I say, I can never drink a black coffee, will I ever drink a black coffee? If I tell myself that I can't learn technology, will I bother trying to learn new technology?

You buy your microphone, and you've got a headset and a nice place to record, along with a website and podcast hosting. You look like a podcaster! You publish your first episode, and that seals the deal—you are a podcaster! You adopt the identity of podcaster. It was as easy and as simple as that. You manifested this new part of your identity.

You can successfully become a podcaster, and at the same time, create additional identities that will make you a happier person, if you wish to be a happier person. As I previously mentioned, you might have to give something up that does not serve you or bring you joy, just to find the time to create a podcast. Therefore, you will no longer identify as a, for example, *Montreal Canadiens fanatic*, or perhaps you will simply take on the identity of *former Montreal Canadiens fanatic*. The latter uses little mental space.

One of the most profound changes that I made to my day-to-day living came with the help of podcasting. I loved what I was doing, and it added layers of meaning to my life. I did find the time to make episodes, but then I needed the optimal time to create. I have 3 young children, and I have a home office. They return from school after 3pm. The youngest is in bed before 9pm. Someone is normally up past 10pm. I don't want to record and disturb anyone.

The best time for me to record has been while everyone sleeps, but I won't stay up past midnight. I tried staying up late at the very beginning of my podcast career, recording late after games, but I felt uncomfortable doing this, and it would always result in a lack of sleep. I determined that early mornings were the only option.

I had tried this in the past, specifically with my meditation practice. When I did, I would fall asleep meditating. I was always exhausted at 5am. I told myself, repeatedly, that it was too early for me, and that was probably why I never succeeded with early mornings.

With the excitement and energy of podcasting, I told myself that I don't have to identify with the guy who *cannot* be an early riser. I told myself that I could, and that it was important to do the podcast. I heard Tony Robbins say something to the effect that it's up to you to have the energy that you want. It's simply a matter of telling yourself, when you open your eyes, to get out of bed, energized, and take on your day.

I then changed that part of my identity and have been a 5am riser almost every day since. I take a walk to get my blood flowing, and then I do something involving my podcast. I am the most productive that I have ever been.

Through the podcast, I stopped identifying myself as shy, which has also been very significant. Podcasting was the tool that I used to do this, somewhat easily. It's like all of the things I wanted to change about myself, or wanted to become, piggy-backed on my podcast, by design and intention.

What have you successfully changed as you have started this podcasting journey? It's never too late for re-identification. It's really about changing your focus, with the help of changing your mind, which you are already a pro at! Podcasting is a positive experience. Here, you can amplify this experience, and create a better version of yourself in the process!

Getting Out of the Shell and Overcoming Shyness

I had been shy for most of my life. I believe that I adopted this shy identity when I was young. Perhaps it fit at the time, and I continued to wear it, up until I became a podcaster. That's a long time!

Grasping onto an identity is something that I had started to realize in my first podcasting year. We see ourselves in a certain way, and because we see certain traits that we possess, we think they are a permanent part of us. There is nothing static about ourselves. We can change our identity, and take on traits and behaviors that serve us.

I have attached the titles of introvert, loner, and shy guy, to my person, for almost my entire life. When I began podcasting, I began to feel a subtle change, and I think it began when I started sharing more about myself. As an entrepreneur, for years, I would make marketing calls, and rarely did I share much of myself. Mostly, my focus was squarely on my client or prospect. My goal was to make the other person feel important. When I was rewarded with business, it was much of the same: learning more about the client's needs, and fulfilling their requirement. I didn't form long-term relationships. In a way, I didn't feel as if I were on equal footing with the executives that I would call upon.

As more of myself came out, with my microphone as the witness, I felt a liberation with sharing my message and story. I could feel an internal shift in the process, and I began to reflect on what was happening. I was an *introvert*. I was often *heavy* or *deep*. Despite recording alone, I was not acting or feeling shy. I questioned myself as to why I was shy in the first place, and where it came from. I could not find the exact time or answer, but I did retrieve some of my earliest shy memories. In these memories, I was often unhappy, and I created the conditions for my own melancholy. I was hurt that I could not join in on the fun with others. I really could have used a coach!

If I created my shyness, or reinforced its existence, could I not take down the wall within my psyche, and build a new one in its place? I simply made the decision to do it.

Podcasting can create the momentum for many things, including overcoming shyness and re-inventing oneself. I simply said that I will no longer associate with my shy identity, and I will leap at any opportunity to socially engage with others. If I am not shy, then I have nothing to fear.

I began networking as much as I could, and got out of my home office. As I started putting myself out there, opportunities arose. I was asked to present to local business groups about podcasting, and I found myself in front of the camera, often. This was a radical shift. As a business owner, between the years of 2005–2016, I might have gone to 2 networking events. As a podcaster, I was aiming for 2 a month.

This simply produced happiness. Feeling alone on a regular basis, or envying groups filled with laughter, does not feed the soul well. It becomes a trap and a cycle, and we accept it, often unable to find the strength to challenge or break it.

Like podcasting, speaking to others is something that improves with practice. I often feel like an awkward teenager, but I know I have something special and unique about me, and within me, as do you, and as we all do.

If you happen to be in this situation, and feel isolation more often than not, you can successfully prescribe the remedy for yourself. It starts with your podcast and allowing yourself to share your stories. Feel that liberation first, and while you feel a sense of freeness, make that determination that you will shed the identities, that quite frankly, don't serve you. As podcasters, we are part of a global community, but we live in a small community, with people around us. You can get a sense of being in a tribe, and a member of a group that accepts you. You are not static. You can and will change, and you are in control of the direction that you want to go.

What Other Podcasters Say About Happiness

"Since I started podcasting in 2008, I've found that it's a really terrific outlet, and it's very rewarding and beneficial. Firstly, it's been great for my practice, helping me position myself as the expert authority in my field, and attracting more good clients and referrals, so I make more money, more easily. That, of course, makes me happy. But it's much more than just that. I'd do all this, even if it lost money. You see, it has given me a platform from which I'm able to give voice to my opinions, views, and advice. It has allowed me to become a teacher and a leader, and perhaps even to inspire some people. Podcasting lets me help others, and that is the ultimate reward."

Gordon Firemark, Attorney at Law
Producer/Host: Entertainment Law Update
Http://entertainmentlawupdate.com

"The *Entrepreneurial You* started as a traditional radio show, in 2014, on a local radio station, in Jamaica. It was profitable, running for three seasons with corporate sponsorship. BUT I knew there was more. Deep inside, there has always been a drive to have a global impact: 'I must move from just desire, to action. There has to be a way.'

Then, seemingly out of nowhere, podcasting presented itself to me. My love affair with this convenient form of content started from a conversation with a Caribbean technology trailblazer. I stated what I wanted to accomplish having a radio show. To cut a long story short, she recommended podcasting as a viable option. That would help me achieve my objective of wanting to reach more people. Eventually, it would become easier to garner sponsorship, if I still wanted to do traditional radio, after I would have developed a large enough online following.

Hooked doesn't begin to explain what happened since I started listening to John Lee Dumas, based on my friend's recommendation. That was in 2016. By the end of March, 2017, with equipment in hand, research on tools software training done, and guests booked and interviewed, I successfully published my podcast in iTunes.

The sense of joy and peace I get from sitting behind a microphone, having a conversation with the most global, high-impact entrepreneurs, is inexplicable. I don't see me stopping anytime soon."

Heneka Watkis-Porter
Creator/Host: The Entrepreneurial You
henekawatkisporter.com

"At first, when I think about the question of how podcasting has made me a happier person, I snort and giggle, as a flood of images run through my mind about this labor of love. At the time we launched *The Department of Understanding Humans*, I was unemployed and full of creative ideas that needed an outlet. My mother had just died; I had left what was supposed to be a budding career as a 9-1-1 dispatcher; and I moved to a different state. Recording, editing, producing… giving birth to this idea in my head; I found my voice. Podcasting is fun and deeply satisfying. It helps me burn off the stress of the week/ month/ year… life. The podcasting community is amazing and supportive; who wouldn't benefit from that? I enjoy the editing process, the art of creating something out of nothing, developing the websites, designing SWAG, and figuring out the next best way to connect with people. The happiness that goes along with it is deep, humble, and filling. Podcasting has, in a sense, made me a happier person: it gave me a new purpose."

Rachel Reese
Founder & Creative Director: The Department of Understanding Humans
www.duhwebsite.com

Let's next explore relationships. We need one another. A Podcast can successfully present opportunities for business and personal relationships. When we have a greater sense of connectedness, we feel less isolated, and enjoy the comfort of acceptance. What follows are the ways that podcasts make this happen.

Chapter 5
New & Enhanced Relationships

"Most people forget that you have to create relationships. The allure of the first years settles down, and at that moment, you better start creating it; otherwise, you're going to lose out."
– John Travolta

I have met others who have no problems whatsoever on creating and establishing relationships with new people. I, on the other hand, have had great difficulty to do this outside of work. The podcast has allowed me to overcome this. If you are now, as I was then, understand that you are fully capable of successfully beginning new friendships, no matter where the other person may be.

Making New Connections

Some will say that podcasting can be an isolating experience. It doesn't have to be. If there is any desire to connect with new people, podcasting is the easy way to do it.

I discovered this with my podcast. I had interviewed podcasters daily on one of my programs. I talked to them before we recorded, and I kept talking to them, well after we had recorded. We create a podcast episode together, but we also take the first steps in getting to know one other. I have met some brilliant and fun people.

There are several ways to connect with other podcasters in this world. Currently, you have an amazing podcast community that will accept you with open arms. You can go to the world's biggest podcast conference, Podcast Movement, smaller conferences and meetups, or you can hang out on Facebook. It will surprise you as to how nice the people are in the podcast community, and how willing they are to help you in any podcast related request, question, or need. If social media is your thing, there are thousands of people eager to connect with you and share the passion of podcasting.

The best way to connect with others through podcasting is to start interviewing people. As I work with podcasters, I simply go onto the Facebook podcast groups, and post a request. For me, it's that easy to make a new connection that I can start a relationship with. Podcasting has been my interest, so I have interviewed podcasters.

This principle and strategy can apply to any niche (see Career & Business in Chapter 7). If you strive for new people to talk to in your life, the first step is to start asking around for guests on your program. Go into the social media platforms, find the people who are interesting, and ask. Some will say no; some will say yes. You might find a flake here and there, but you can weed them out early on. Perhaps you will need to leave your comfort zone when you make the initial request, but once you have left your comfort zone, and it pays off, that is where the personal growth begins.

I've made new friends. Despite not living within my community, Skype connects us live in real time. We have common interests, and I genuinely care about my new friends. When I speak to them, I am only interested in them, their accomplishments, and the fun that they are having with their podcast. This fulfills a relationship need for me, outside family and my business. It provides greater substance, in comparison to social media likes and new friend requests, which only seems to provide moments of artificial satisfaction.

If you podcast on sports, bring on a guest who also shares your passion. You'll find all of these folks on Twitter. If you are in business, reach out to potential partners, or people within the industry, who you can't necessarily work directly with. Find someone who knows more than you, and ask them to be on your show. Stay in touch with everyone you like. When you do a podcast episode together, you have already created the beginnings to a bond. It's amazing!

Prior to podcasting, I made thousands of phone calls in the pursuit of closing sales. There are but a small handful that I still connect with.

The industry I was in tends to be negative. In the employment world, people are hired, fired, get new managers, sign up for something that was not initially told to them (in the job description and interview), and are often told to do more than what they are capable of doing. I have created wonderful beginnings with many, but it never ends wonderfully for them, unless they quit and start their own business. The antidote, should I have remained, would have been a podcast, and a regular feeding of happy people wanting to make a difference. It you are in a negative work industry, a podcast can help with creating better balance.

I am at the point, that if I need to talk, I can always find someone to connect with. It's amazing. There are so many great people in the world that you would have never known, if it weren't for your podcast interviews. If you wish to expand yourself, start interviewing people from time to time. You can expand the circle of the people in your life, and create more friendships. I have been very successful with this, despite not intentionally seeking friends. It's right there for you too.

Podcasters Around the World

Through my podcast, I have talked to people in Canada, the United States, the Caribbean, Sweden, Australia, England, Germany, Ireland, and China. In the old days, if I wanted to talk to people outside my country, I would have had to leave the soil. Of course, the advantage to this would be sightseeing, and the security of tourism, but if you wanted to meet a local, in a non-threatening way (for either party), that could be a bit difficult without any introduction. The podcast is a great introduction.

In a way, it's like traveling, without history and flight. I love connecting with those who live overseas. When I have traveled to different parts of the world, I would look at the locals and think that there was very little difference between us, besides culture. The locals were doing their best to live their lives, care for their family, and fill themselves up with the interests that provide them with happiness and satisfaction. I determined that we all had common struggles.

When you talk to another podcaster on the other side of the pond (as my friend, Ian Farrar, from the *Industry Angel Business* podcast, would say), you really can understand the sameness that we all share, minus the politics, and perhaps oppression. As of this writing, I am on the hunt for a Russian podcaster who speaks English. I suspect that there is not much different from myself and a North Korean. Just thinking about this helps me to reflect on how I have won the lottery of life.

This planet we inhabit is a small place. It did not feel like this when I took an airplane, for 24 hours, to China, but when I connect with people around the world through my podcast, it certainly does. There is an advantage to seeing things this way, without distance. It's a matter of connectedness. When this began for me, I was overtaken by this strange sense that the world was talking to me through the many voices scattered throughout the planet. In a way, it felt as though it were one voice. Perhaps this is where the phrase, *one world, one voice*, comes from. It was a brief but very profound, spiritual feeling.

This feeling, insight, realization, or whatever you would like to call it, came out of the process of podcasting. This is my own individual experience, which may not reflect well in written word, but the possibility might exist for you.

Have you achieved anything like this through your podcast? Do you believe in this possibility? The first step is to start interviewing people on your podcast, and then be open to those who sound and speak differently than you. When I started this, I worried about understanding others with strong accents, but I quickly realized that this was a barrier that I fictitiously created. Once I ignored it, the fun began.

A Great Way to Connect With Those Whom You Admire

As I was joyfully plugging away at my podcast, I did struggle with obsessively thinking about things to podcast on. *Writers get blocks.* I'd say Podcasters do too. I always managed to come up with something daily. Some of it was good. Some of it was okay. Some of it was excellent. When I thought it was bad, I would listen to the show afterwards and think that it was not bad after all.

I needed more than my monologues. At that point, my old program was about being motivated and living a good life at work, and outside work. I was not yet the Podcaster's Coach, with podcasting friends. I heard, within the Facebook podcast communities, if you wanted to attract more listeners, then you should start interviewing others. They will share your podcast with their *tribe,* and this could result in new subscribers.

I thought about this, and asked myself, "Who would I want to interview? Who would I want to talk to? Of course, Lama Marut!"

Lama Marut, aka Brian K. Smith, started the *Lama Marut Podcast,* in 2007, and it remains active. I mentioned Lama Marut's one podcast episode that helped me change my life. I absorbed as much as I could and, eventually, became a Buddhist. Lama Marut was my hero and inspiration back then; so much so, I traveled from Toronto to Vancouver, to participate in a weekend retreat. It was a silent retreat, and I never spoke to him.

As the years passed, my Buddhism became a little cloudier, or I became less fanatical. I had turned my spiritual studies into a job and, in turn, I was neglecting everything else. I suppose I jumped on the *easy path* afterwards by studying much less but still maintaining a Buddhist worldview, along with gratitude for all that I learned from all of the teachers that I had been exposed to.

I decided that I would ask Lama Marut to be on my podcast as my first ever guest. Surely, he would not have the time for me! I was incredibly nervous about putting myself in a position for rejection.

Maybe it sounds funny that the person who I wanted to connect most with, on the entire planet, was a former Buddhist monk. These are personal choices, of course. Maybe yours is an athlete, a celebrity, an activist, or a political reformer. Just go and ask. Make a list. Go one by one, until someone agrees. Someone will agree, if you approach them tactfully, with sincerity and courtesy.

Lama Marut did agree! I interviewed him over Skype, and it was a thrill. I was a terrible interviewer, but like the podcast itself, it has greatly improved over time. I am much better now—absolutely.

The podcast was a very easy way to connect with someone whom I admired. It was a reason to talk. Could I have contacted Lama Marut, and said, "Brian, I would love to have a conversation with you. Can we have a phone call so I can learn more?" I suppose I could have done this, but would he have agreed to that? Most people would think that I was a little nuts. Of course, if you ask to have a phone conversation with someone you admire, and they happen to have products and services to sell, you might get that phone call.

I did a few others afterward: Shree (who I had personally learned a great deal from), Sam Crowley (a successful early adapter podcaster), and Raymond Aaron. I had agreements with others who had written wonderful books and were backing very worthy causes, but I ultimately canceled these, as my podcast was going through a change, and I was following my passion to move toward being an Influencer in the podcasting community and industry.

I discovered, long ago, that most people are kind, even those with greater popularity and celebrity. If you ask, and you get declined, consider that the timing might not have been right. After all, you are very busy too. We live in a world of busyness. We can't all say yes to everything.

You can do this. If and when you do, you will interview people you admire. Most people will never have these types of conversations. You have, or you will!

Common Interests With Family Members

The potential is there to strengthen relationships with those in your family. I have talked to podcasters who podcast with their parents, and I think that this is amazing. I have daydreamed about podcasting with my father, and how it would give us so much more in common, when we presently have little in common. I still have not managed to get my father to use the Whatsapp messaging app on his phone, so forget about a podcast!

I had plenty in common with my cousin, Albert, and we did my first podcast together. It was called *The Habs Life*. Despite me doing 99% of the work, his participation made it easier for me to start. Perhaps I was seeing it as a safer process for my very first episode, as I was podcasting with a loved one.

Our show lasted 12 episodes, but it was interesting to see and feel this new added element to our relationship. We could talk for hours about comics when we were kids growing up in Montreal, as well as our extended family, hockey, soccer, and movies, and now we can add our podcast to that. It seemed to extend our range for conversation. I could feel in my heart that my podcasting passion was something that I could turn into a career, and it was very nice to start off in the learning trenches with my cousin.

Our podcast did not work out, as the theme of the podcast—hockey— was not fitting for my lifestyle of positivity (and early mornings). It was something that I enjoyed to watch, but too much of it became consuming. I wanted to be consumed with living a positive, motivated, and happy life, not by a sport with the occasional violence that I had a hard time being a witness too. Watching grown men on skates, wearing body armor, and occasionally hitting another in the head, always left me gasping.

The key to doing a successful podcast, with a co-host, is to ensure in advance that the podcast does not interfere in the relationship. The podcast requires a game plan and shared duties. It does not have to require endless hours. Just decide what the theme is, how often to record, who is responsible for the episode topic, show notes, scheduling, editing, and sharing. It does not have to be a huge production. What's most important is sharing something together and having fun.

Next, is a theme that I discovered on my own, and quickly learned that I was not alone in its discovery: podcasting as a form of self-therapy.

Chapter 6
Self Help & Podcast Pseudo Therapy

"One way to feel good about yourself is to love yourself... to take care of yourself." – Goldie Hawn

This was most unsuspected. Over time, I became lighter. I let things go that I didn't realize were holding me back. The podcast began to resemble a much needed friend. When the episodes were done, I felt like a better person.

Putting Yourself Out There

For many of us, it takes a lot of initial courage to get personal while podcasting. Your personality will come out, and no matter what you discuss, personal pieces of you will come out. If you podcast solo, this will absolutely happen.

I first heard the term, *Audible Diary*, from Joe, from the *Potentium Podcast*, when I had him on my program. For him, what was most important was to get *out* all of his thoughts and ideas from the past week, release them, and turn them into content for his weekly program, which also is a family affair that includes his brother Ed. It doesn't matter if he has 2 listeners, or 200. For him, it's a need and an outlet to get things off his mind.

There is a sort of liberation when you podcast. As scary as it might seem at first, it does feel good to get things off your mind, using the physical microphone as your non-judgemental listener. I felt this many times in my podcasting, when I didn't expect it.

When I was in my 20s, I worked in a restaurant as an office manager, bartender, and waiter. At the time, it was the best job I ever had, with a really terrific owner, Alex. With any business, people come and go, and the restaurant hired a talented chef but a very nasty person, at times. I found it unbearable to work in this new environment, and I decided to resign. I was in need of a new living arrangement (which also played a part in my resignation), but I never told any of this to Alex. He was disappointed that I was leaving; he flat out told me that he was not getting my full story but accepted that I was moving on. I stayed longer than I wanted but finally worked my last day. It was the only job that I have ever had that I hold dear, as an employee. It was a time and place where I grew leaps and bounds as a person.

Twenty years went by, and this came out in a podcast. I had been holding onto feelings of regret all of that time, and I didn't even know it. I explained the situation, the details around it, apologized to Alex for not being 100% honest, and extended a heartfelt gratitude for the overall experience.

The result of this 3-minute portion of my podcast was a feeling of relief, and a release of something unhealthy in my subconscious, however minor it may have been. I seem to have granted myself a sense of freedom and joy. I hope that I experience this again.

I have heard podcasters do the same by sharing experiences of their lives. I listen to at least 25 new podcasts a month, and perhaps a quarter of the ones I hear have the host sharing something personal. Sometimes it is heavy, like abuse, and other times, a little lighter, like dishonesty. I know that they feel a sense of release when they put themselves out there. The beautiful thing about it is that most say they do it in order to help others through their life examples.

The first time I did this intentionally, I questioned myself long and hard about putting myself out there, and sharing something personal that I have not shared before to any living soul. It's not that I do not trust others with these details. It's more about not needing to share these moments, or the necessity to share them in regular conversation.

Perhaps our past becomes present, or more accessible, when we are in a creative mind frame. I don't know.

There is the boundary that you step through when it comes to sharing. You move from the space that you can look behind with your personal stories, then you take a step forward, over a line, to where your microphone stands. It's scary as you step over the boundary, loaded with an assortment of feelings, like fear, courage, apprehension, and strength. What follows next, after it sets in, is a sense of importance.

People put themselves *out there* all of the time with social media, and most of the time, it's written. There is something much more profound with the voice, loaded with inflection, feeling, and warmth.

Does putting yourself out there even qualify as a component of success? I get the sense that I am a better person after doing this. I think I have lived more successfully after doing this. I cannot prove it, but if I reflect on the lessons that I have shared, or the pain that I let go of in my podcast, I get a sense that some of my past may have been slowing me down in some ways. I love the sense of feeling lighter.

Liberating The Pain Within – Release & Teach

There was an episode where I seemed to settle, or close, a chapter of my life that was painful—pain that was not consciously present in my day to day living. It was an amazing, liberating experience, and I doubt I would have experienced it, if it were not for my podcast.

It began in the form of writing. My episodes were scripted at the time. My process was to write, rehearse, adjust, and then record. I had been working on my legacy project at the time, and the day before my episode, I had recorded a video of myself, explaining details of old photographs that I have saved of myself and my family. This was fresh on my mind, and it would make a good episode.

What eventually released, was pain. I didn't want it, but it was there, so rather than repress, I let it go. I rarely think of my childhood or spend much time in my past. I have really tried hard to keep present, as I don't know how accurate my past thoughts are anymore. The future, I know, is fiction. *The time is now*, is one of my favorite mantras.

There was some chaos in my life as a child. It came from my father who, unfortunately, I remember as being mostly an angry person. There are some pleasant memories from my childhood of him, but they are few and far between. Our relationship is good today, but it required forgiveness and compassion— perhaps the two greatest tools for a happy life.

Eventually, my mother had had enough of the environment, and she left him, with myself, and my little brother and sister. It was a courageous move that improved our lives instantly, but it was a bumpy road for a long time, until all of our lives settled. When I look at my own young children, I rejoice that they are living the life of children, and are not stressed or burdened with adult problems being thrust upon them.

I went through many photographs of a fractured family. The pictures themselves displayed happiness, yet there was a hidden layer of sadness in many of them. It reminded me of the difficult childhood I had— the intimidation, the harshness, and the control—all of it beyond my child-self's intellectual comprehension. It was like becoming that child again, witnessing the past again, with greater wisdom and less confusion.

The podcast episode set my pain free. The thoughts began to form with my writing, and they were let go with my voice. It was a bit hard to do because my mind thought that I might be making a mistake telling this to the public, but the world—the planet, Mother Nature, the source, or whatever you want to call it— could also be the witness of healing. In a funny way, the world also heals itself in the process.

I felt much lighter, and then I moved on. It felt finished. Over. Done. Resolved in a way. It was a part of my path. I am here now, still moving forward toward self-actualization, happily.

Through the process of putting a podcast episode together, I successfully came to terms with a painful period in my past, doing so in a healthy way. I am better than I was before. I successfully put a hard time behind me. I honestly don't' know of others who have had this exact experience as a podcaster, but I do know of others who have rejoiced in the release of good memories, and even bad ones.

I am not advocating for podcasters to publish all of the terrible things that have happened to them, but if a podcaster wants to help others who might have gone through the same thing, the podcast can both release and teach. It's a tool to dig into yourself more deeply, and to help others not feel so alone.

Use an Audible Diary

I have begun to see more podcasters using a podcast to transform themselves, change their habits, and reinvent themselves. It is on the rise because it works.

I talked about my experience with de-identifying and re-identifying myself. When you podcast, you focus on the subject and topic. If you want a more positive life, you create a regular podcast about the positive things in life. You ultimately get what you give. If you want more complaining, keep complaining. If you want more happiness, share more happiness.

This came true for me. It wasn't difficult, nor was it forced. It was simply a matter of focus; and then, organically, my life improved because I wanted to help others improve. I took everything that I knew, and shared it. If I had an idea about something, I learned more about it, and then I shared it. Podcasters crave for feedback and engagement. I would be lying to you if I said that I helped many people, but I knew that people were listening, simply by reading my statistics. It had to have made an impact somewhere to someone.

The concept of recording a daily podcast to create a new life for yourself is brilliant. When I see it, I tell myself that that podcaster is undergoing something special. I may attempt it down the road, but I am happy to join the others on their ride. After all, it's free wonderful content.

I journaled and kept a diary for close to 10 years when in my 20s. I often had great difficulty with other people (including difficulty with living with myself), and I found it very useful to write it all out. I simply needed it out, and it felt like a healthy thing to do.

The journals collected dust in my basement for a very long time, and when I decided to de-clutter and simplify, they all had to go. When I reread them, I wanted to be sure of what I was doing; after all, there were a lot of memories in these books. What I found was a lot of negativity, and at times, repetitive negativity. I recalled many of the situations that I wrote about, but they were not memories that I could place any value on for the present time. Then I questioned if this could be useful somehow, perhaps for my children. I could not see it. I simply found every written or half written poem, tore them out, and recycled everything else. It all almost seemed like a waste, but surely it had some value to me back then.

What happened, in these journals, is that I continued to get what I focused on. The journal proved it, as I was often saying the same thing, over and over. As the journal, or diary, can be the place holder for the negative (in cases like mine), the podcast can hold the potential of positive change.

It is long overdue to have a medium to combat the nightly 6pm news. The so-called *news* always reports tragedy and suffering, and shares so few of the stories of the amazing people in the world, or in our community. Amazing people are all around us. It's no wonder why we don't seek eye contact. It's no wonder we struggle with random acts of kindness. It's no wonder we don't trust anyone. What's depicted in the news, on TV and radio, is a terrible world, which people believe exists. I rejoice in the day when all cars have Apple Podcasts, and it becomes incredibly easy to consume the messages that inspire us, and not frighten us.

If you want to successfully change, podcast your personal growth, with regularity. You can do that free, too, if you use a micro podcasting service (short podcast duration form). It's so easy to do this. You can create the life that you want. You can talk about what you want to do with your life. You can record and listen back. You can track your progress. You can understand what you need to do differently. You can try, and try again, and again, and again, until you get what you want.

Your podcast is absolutely not a replacement for professional help if you need it. Myself, and others, have found it a great help to feel better about ourselves, when we need to feel better about ourselves. This may or may not work for all, but I suspect that even If a podcaster does not set their intention on self- therapy through the podcast, they might just get it.

This book would not be complete if I didn't include monetary wealth. Podcasting has become an occupation for some on a full-time or part-time basis. Podcasts have become an important and effective tool for content marketing. It can also, absolutely, be used to enhance a career and job search. The next chapter offers much of what I have learned about this since becoming the Podcaster's Coach.

Chapter 7
Career, Business, and Income

"The greatest ability in business is to get along with others and to influence their actions." – John Hancock

Podcasts are incredibly powerful. They are capable of allowing you to create your authority, easily. They can move you into the direction of prosperity and/or career change. They can make working, better. And, of course, they can create a highly desired alternative revenue stream.

Those Who Listen to You, Will Believe You

After I began my career as the Podcaster's Coach—and no one ever told me that I was not a Podcaster's Coach—my school actually granted me a second certification as a *Podcaster's Coach*, to go along with my Certified Professional Life Coach Certificate. The ICF (International Coaching Federation) granted me membership, so I was ready with a rebuttal for anyone who wished to challenge me. It has never happened, and at this point, I doubt it ever will.

In a way, I received a stamp of approval from the podcast community by not receiving any criticism from them. For the most part, podcasters are a happy group, so I am in the right space.

No one has ever criticized me. No one has ever told me that I am not a coach. No one has ever said that I had no right to call myself the *Podcaster's Coach*. No one has even hid behind a social media account to challenge me or put me down.

Perhaps I have missed negative comments somewhere? I don't feed negativity to my mind. Social media is full of it, and I have become very selective on what I look at. If there is a tone of complaining or attack, I don't get involved, and I don't give bad comments or opinions another second of attention. Actually, I rarely see it anymore, since I mostly only pay attention to what the podcast community is saying. They are a helpful group, not a hurtful group.

The people I have interviewed confirmed that I am the *Podcaster's Coach*. They have referred to me as the *Podcaster's Coach*. The *Podcaster's Coach* is in the show title, and guests still come on my program. Each day that passes, and each show that I produce, further strengthens my foundation.

People have always believed who I said I was. People have listened to me. I seem to have been accepted at the very start. Only two months after taking the title, *Podcaster's Coach,* I was accepted as a featured speaker for International Podcast Day™. John Lee Dumas, who might be the most well-known Podcaster in the world, presented hours after me, with his co-presenter, Gary Leland. How incredible was that? Yes, I was beaming!

I can only assume that those who allowed me to present, had listened to my podcast, checked out my website, and tracked me on social media. I must have done enough, and I didn't do much. I was anticipating a *no* on my presentation submission, but what I received was a most welcomed *yes.*

If you podcast, and if people listen to you with regularity, they will believe you. No one will want to listen to you if they think you are a liar. If you wish to become something, and share what you honestly know, no matter how much you know, you will begin to develop credibility and trust with your audience.

This is incredibly powerful when it comes to starting a business, looking for a new career, or wishing to become a thought leader on a topic. Human beings seek approval. Podcasting is a way to successfully receive approval. At its simplest, the numbers of listeners will point you in that direction. Perhaps you cannot see the faces that approve of you and your message, but even if a few do, then you have the ears that are attached to the minds. As you keep going, you increase your audience of trust. It's a wonderful feeling, if you want it. You can also plan the hopes of income around it. It's slow for most, and fast for others, but one of the biggest buying traits is trust, and you can build that through your podcast.

Becoming a Public Speaker

Podcasters are public speakers. Perhaps the audience is unknown, but the process is present while recording. When I scripted my podcast, I found that the process was very similar.

The big differences are rehearsal and physical appearance. You can be an unkempt or unshaven, pajama- wearing podcaster, but you need to look your best in front of an audience. Presenters cannot read, but a podcaster can script without sounding like reading. Besides that, a podcaster who wishes to include or transition into public speaking can do so with some extra effort but relative ease.

When I began speaking as the *Podcaster's Coach*, this was new territory for me. I did not know what I was doing for my first speaking gig, and I was a body full of nervous energy, leading up to the event. I received 2 pieces of amazing advice. First, approach it at 85% (thank you Gary). Wanting to be a perfect presenter was a big source of my anxiety. I did not want to come across as a fool or look foolish. I wanted to be spot on and make the best impression possible. Being told to approach it at 85% was also great advice for aspiring or new podcasters. Instead of going crazy, trying to create the best first podcast episode of all time, which can often lead to procrastination, just go in at 85%, because your first podcast episode, when you listen to it a year from now, will suck. Why should public speaking be any different from podcasting? Once I took that 100% perfection off the table, and decided to be less than perfect, it took almost all of the pressure off.

The next best piece of advice that I received was to remember that I knew what I was talking about, and not to overburden myself with presentation memorization. I was speaking for an hour, and my approach was to write the entire speech out and memorize it line by line. Talk about making myself miserable! This was not the best approach to take, and I was making myself crazy. I was told to stop doing this, and to remember that I am the subject matter expert, and it's not necessary to memorize the entire speech. I already knew the material. I just had to say it.

At this point, with these tools in your back pocket, if you wish to become a public speaker (which I think is a natural progression for the podcaster), you may have to tangle with *Impostor Syndrome,* briefly. Luckily, my battle was brief.

I cannot tell you where Impostor Syndrome comes from, or why it attacks us. Public speaking and podcasting are both fun and enjoyable activities. I can only explain it from the perspective of having a natural negative mind. The mind attaches to negative thoughts like Velcro, and to positive thoughts like Teflon. Maybe it's just a natural struggle to remain in a state of happiness and joy. When you undertake an activity that can lead to joy and happiness, the mind will not make it easy for the individual. Perhaps it wants to attach itself to the ideas of unworthiness, and being undeserving, incapable, and unacceptable.

If you are a podcaster, and you podcast on a topic, you know the topic. Even if you have only 3 podcast episodes on a topic, then you know the topic much more than others do. Perhaps you are not a complete expert, but you know enough to get started. You are becoming the person you set out to be, and you use the podcast, and opportunities to speak in front of groups, to further strengthen your capabilities and your new improved identity.

I love the opportunity to speak; rarely, I decline a chance to do it. I want people to see what I see. If I can get their attention, then I will try my best to show them the benefits of podcasting.

This also reminds me of an idea that is spread throughout the podcasting community. As a podcaster, you may have 25 people that listen to your podcast regularly. The podcaster that sees this as a failure is mistaken. Having 25 regular listeners is like speaking to an audience of 25 people who are interested in your message. This is a great opportunity to make an impact on the lives of others. It's something to cherish, practice, and increase the level of your authority as a thought leader in the area of your choosing.

Branding Yourself With a Podcast

When it occurred to me that I had the passion and desire to become the *Podcaster's Coach*, I realized that I could begin to brand myself this way, effortlessly, because there was no other. There were podcast coaches, but my uniqueness was not on the technical part alone; it was a combination of both technical and personal.

The longer that I am the *Podcaster's Coach*, the stronger my brand becomes, as long as I keep myself visible and relevant. This book may improve my brand persona. They say everyone has a book in them. If I can do this, you can do this too.

Podcasting is a simple and easy way to brand. Your beginning, if you are unique, will be easy. Cover all of the areas of the internet: Facebook, Twitter, Instagram, and LinkedIn social media handles, along with an URL. The hardest part of all of this is finding your uniqueness, but you have it in you. Take the time you need to put it into words.

Next, the podcast—take the name before someone else does. Even if you are the first, you cannot have ownership by simply having a podcast named after your brand, unless you own the exclusive legal rights. Perhaps more podcaster coaches will appear, doing exactly what I am doing. I brand myself as the world's first authentic

Podcaster's Coach, and I have the history and experience to prove it. Regardless, if I could inspire more podcaster coaches, I would be both equally honored and supportive.

The longer I go, the more often I am referred to as *Coach*. It's amazing.

A podcaster can successfully begin a brand, the same way I started mine. Take your passion, know what you are going to do or sell, create a memorable name that accurately describes you, and then start building your credibility and visibility by podcasting. Of course, figure out what your value proposition is, and absolutely know who your buyers and listeners are. I've heard the term, *avatar,* several times. Create your podcast avatar. The avatar is the person who buys from you and listens to you. They are fictitious, but your best example of someone who listens to you. Give them a name, with features and behaviors. Go deep with the character. Where do they live and what do they do with their spare time? What do they do for a living? How big is their family? And on, and on. Understand what fuels their decision-making. This is some basic information for you to consider and explore for your podcast and business. Do it all for your avatar.

Podcasting can open the door for the brand awareness path. You will find listeners, you can create content through your podcast, you can interview other professionals who will instantly accept you if they agree, and you can begin by building your brand on a foundation of trust and value, if you are honest and giving.

I remember talking to a person, around the same age as myself, about branding. We talked about childhood experiences, and professional wrestling came up (it was crazy popular in the 80s). The easiest and simplest way I could explain branding to them, was by talking about *gimmicks.* Wrestlers have gimmicks. "Give yourself one as well," I said, "But remove any negative connotation with the word, *gimmick.*" Look for a name that best describes what you do, who you are, what you value, and what your listeners will understand, be drawn to, and

resonate with. Hulk Hogan used to say his prayers, eat his vitamins, and stand up against those who put his country down. He was beloved, he developed his brand, and sold tons of merchandise!
Be interesting. Be direct. Be true to yourself.

It's all about visibility afterwards. Podcast, post, connect, repeat. Turn your podcast content into a 5- minute video. Transcribe a show, and create a blog post. Repurpose or diversify—whatever works for you. Get out there; tell the world who you are, and what your message can do for others, and keep on marketing. Your brand awareness will get amplified if you interview those with a large following. Once they share your podcast with their tribe, it gives you greater potential for exposure, list building, and sales. Just make sure you know what people want.

Podcasting monetary success can be a long road. Stick with your podcast, and pump out the online content. You already started a speaking career, yes? Go out there and speak. Raise your visibility. Speak at online summits, and get out in your community. Always look for speaking engagements. Give as much value as you possibly can.

Chances are, within your community, there may not be many people podcasting in your niche. You can quickly become that podcasting guy within your community. I've talked to people who did this, and the community asked for their help in getting their own podcast started. Before long, new businesses were formed helping others, and getting paid, with podcast production.

That is all it really takes to get started branding yourself. Podcasting is an easy and highly effective way to do it. Get your angle, your tag line, your value proposition, and your uniqueness, and get building a new reputation for the life that you have been dreaming about for so long.

They Will Buy From You First

As entrepreneurs, you are dropping the ball by not creating a podcast. Many years ago, businesses started creating websites. A lot of people said that it was a waste of time. They were wrong. Your business must have a website. These days, you have to do so many things around a website to be relevant and found.

People might tell you that you don't need a podcast, like they did when the websites first appeared. What if they are wrong, like those people back then who said you didn't need a website?

Are we all looking for a competitive advantage right now? I am!

My family lives just outside Toronto, in a small community called Durham Region. I have realized that people here take their time to buy. At times, it might take you multiple conversations to close a sale. Imagine this: you meet someone new, your conversation ends, and they ask you for a business card; on it, you show them the small section about your podcast. They are interested in podcasts and want to know more about them. You give them a quick overview and direct them to your mobile friendly website. You suggest that they give it a listen on their commute back home. Your new acquaintance decides to skip the bad news on the local radio and listen to your podcast instead. They listen to you, they learn more about your product or service, and they get to know you better.

If they need or want what you offer as a product or service, how much more likely are they to buy from you over someone else? Did the odds improve after they have listened to your podcast? If you have created a friendly, honest, value-driven podcast, then yes, of course, you will stick out!

Let's say you own a *brick and mortar*. Imagine that you leave your podcast details on the counter, and a non-buyer notices, picks up your card, and then listens later. Do you think that they might come back to your store after they have listened to your podcast? Is it more likely that they might choose your store over another? If you had a pleasant helpful interaction with your potential customer, they might be motivated to listen.

These scenarios are not farfetched. Creating a podcast separates you from your competition. As podcasters, we are all responsible for educating others on what podcasts are, and how to consume them. People are genuinely interested in podcasts, even if they don't know anything about them. Imagine turning a prospect on to the world of podcasts. They will get hooked on the medium, and they will probably never forget you.

Just in case you might not have yet started your business podcast, here's the good news: podcasting is not hard. As a **bonus** for purchasing this book, please go to www.TheBookOnPodcasting.com, and receive a substantial discount on the *Startup Podcast Program,* which I offer consultants and aspiring entrepreneurs who wish to get their podcast started quickly, with assistance and help. The program offers the opportunity to be part of the Business Podcast Network, and a Podcaster Mastermind.

Alternatively, you can simply watch some YouTube videos, or copy some of the other formulas from other business related podcasts. Really, there are no rules. Ultimately, like a good business, you approach your podcast with professionalism and value. Just ensure that you inject your personality, and that you are being yourself, and not trying to be someone else.

If you love your business, if you love helping others, if you are focused and motivated, and you love your industry, you will never run out of material. Talking to your customers will inspire and direct your content.

Podcasting is a new marketing strategy, and the market is not saturated. Very few people in my community podcast. If they do, they are dropping the ball on visibility. Business podcasts are growing but at a slow pace. The arrow is moving up. It is absolutely a great time to start your podcast now!

If anyone spends their time to listen to your message, they will begin to trust you, and in a strange way, consider you a friend. We tune out to those who we think are untrustworthy. A business podcast can become an extension of yourself, a reflection of your brand, and an advertisement for your products or services.

Do Podcast, Don't Blog

It will sound strange when I say that people don't read (especially since you are reading), or rather, I should say, people don't read as much as they used to. Perhaps it's the new generations that read less? Or maybe it's just a reflection of society and our culture of busyness. We just lack the time to do a lot of reading.

Blogging used to be a big thing, but it has been trending downward for some time now. Videos remain very popular, and podcasts continue to trend upwards.

Blogging is a great way to create content for your website, and help with your webpage authority and Google rankings, but podcasting can do the same, yet be more effective because people will actually listen to your podcast. Ask yourself, "Will my prospects, fans, or my avatar listen, or read?" What is easier for them to do in their busy schedule?

Don't get me wrong, I absolutely adore writing. When I couple writing and podcasting, I feel amazing inside. I love the writing process and the creativity of word selection. I nerd out with words and their meanings. It always feels good to me when I expand my vocabulary.

A podcast can do everything a blog can do, and more. You can write a blog post, and then create an audio recording in a short amount of time. You can double your pleasure: post your blog, and also give someone the option to listen to it. By creating an audio version, you can make it very easy for your followers to consume your content. They won't have to load up your website on their web browser if they are challenged for time. They can simply hear your message from the podcast player on their mobile phone. Look around and see all the people on their mobile phone. We are all focused on the technology that fits into our pocket.

Do both. Create a blog post, and then a day or two after, publish your podcast with the same content. Create a blog post that showcases your podcast episode. Your episode will be on iTunes and Apple Podcasts, and your website as well. Can a written blog post do that?

I have heard podcasters who, when they record, sound as if they are reading. That's okay to start. If someone sets their intention (of not sounding like a reader), with a little practice, it will sound more spontaneous and free flowing. I used to script a 20-minute episode, and I read the entire time while recording. I felt more confident doing it this way. When I engaged with family and friends who told me that they listened, I asked them if they could tell if I was reading. They always said no. It seemed like I was the only one who knew.

Double down: create your blog, or post your article, but podcast as well. If you advertise on your website, you can also advertise on your podcast. There are no rules.

It is a bit sad that we don't read as often as we used to. Perhaps technology has created so many distractions that it has altered our attention span. It is what it is, and if you agree and understand, then it's time for an improved approach.

Let me expand on the one distinct advantage, in the next section, of what podcasts possess over both blogging and video. It's the magic of portability.

Your Message Consumed Just About Everywhere

Podcasts are portable. At this time of writing, they are mostly consumed from mobile phones. We're all a little naked without our phones. Podcasts are practically following people around.

Podcasts can be listened to just about anywhere. I listen to podcasts when I do the laundry, clean the house, go for a walk, do the dishes, make supper, during my run, at the gym, and in my car. You can't do these things and read a blog at the same time. I have found myself loading a video, turning off the screen, and treating it like a podcast, but it's time consuming, and I can't do that when I am busy. All it takes to listen to a podcast is to download a simple podcast player, add your shows, and make sure that your streams are updated, which requires a simple adjustment to your settings. That's it! There is very little to it.

The popularity of podcasts will explode once vehicles are equipped with podcast players. The technology in cars will make it so much easier to consume when we drive. It's not really hard now, when you think of it. My podcast player is loaded with shows, and when I turn my car on, the Bluetooth connects with my device right away, and then my podcast plays automatically, right where I left off from the podcast that I was listening to.

Having a *podcast player button* in our cars will reprogram our driving radio habits. When I turn on the radio, songs play that I don't like, talk radio broadcasts something I find uninteresting, and the commercials are incredibly annoying. I can't count the amount of times when I turned on the radio in the middle of a commercial. I turn it off right away.

People must still listen to the radio because businesses are still spending money on radio ads. It seems crazy to me. One thing I love about podcasts is that I can listen to an episode for 30 minutes, and perhaps 1–2 of those minutes are from sponsors. I have heard some podcasts where it sounds like the entire show is an advertisement. My simple solution is to unsubscribe and find something better to add to my rotation.

Podcasts let you choose what you want to listen to that most interests you. Radio offers very little choice. I suppose you could plan your busy schedule around radio programming, but that sounds ridiculous, doesn't it? The smarter radio stations are now turning their popular segments and shows into podcasts after they air, minus the countless minutes of advertising.

And honestly, do people like to be subjected to seemingly non-stop radio ads? I canceled my TV cable package many years ago. I thought that they should be giving cable away for free, as consumers are subjected to endless commercials. Cable television should be free. Buy my viewing time with your advertisements—sounds better, no? Podcasts and video streaming have it right by offering a much better balanced and acceptable exchange.

Your audience will most likely not stop their jog to fast forward your 30-second sponsorship podcast ad. Podcast listeners are not offended, as they understand that they are getting free content. Cable companies, on the other hand, get little sympathy from their subscribers.

It all goes back to our busy schedules and not having the time to do all the things we want to do. Podcasts are highly enjoyable, and podcast listeners love their podcasts. With a podcast, a listener can do two things at once: perform a task that requires little focus, and wear ear buds. It's a great way to expand our interests by listening and learning from others.

There are people out there who will be interested in what you have to say and offer. Once they find you, then they can take you wherever they go. It's a medium, in this regard, far superior to the others.

Business Development & Lead Generation

The podcast is a tool for business. It creates brand awareness; it should be value driven, and it has the ability to attract prospects.

Think of it as a business card on a large dose of steroids.

I've already talked about face to face networking, and the brick and mortar store scenarios. You can add cold calling to the list, if you market this way. I do this, as it's been the most inexpensive way to get new clients. I've done a lot of cold calling; many times, I would be told by the prospect to email the information or a brochure. Sometimes that is the way for the prospect to say *go away*. Instead of a brochure, why not include your latest podcast in the email? Or, if you have managed to have a short conversation with the prospect, and if there was something that came up that was already a topic on one of your podcast episodes, make it stand out in the email. This is a wonderful way for you to stand out too.

When *follow-ups* or *checking-in* emails are sent, again, there are more opportunities to send the relevant and most desired podcast episode. Perhaps in the previous phone call, and short conversation, a topic came up, and it inspired you to create content. You follow up, a month later, and mention how they inspired your show! You share the episode and thank them. They could ignore it, they can listen to it, or they could subscribe for later listening. Let the podcast keep you at the top of their mind. Again, when anyone listens to a podcast, and they keep listening, they develop trust for the speaker. Trust is key when it comes to buying and entering into a business relationship.

If you know what your prospects struggle with, and what they need, this should reflect the bulk of your business podcast. If you can touch all of the pain points of the industry, and show your uniqueness, you will have a business development tool that makes you stand out from the rest of the competition.

In the event where you are very niche, creating a podcast around your business helps your prospects find you. The podcast will help you get found by those looking for what you have to offer. The more content, the greater the chance to be found. The podcast gives you an additional layer of exposure, and podcast players can act like search engines. The more podcasts grow in popularity, the greater amount of *searches* transpire. Is it crazy to imagine a prospect wanting to know more about the industry, finding you, liking you, and reaching out? Maybe this is uncommon for most, but for the very niche, I would say it is not.

Podcasts can be a lead generation magnet, no matter what the market. If you have something that someone wants, and they like your message, then they will explore you further. This works for the most popular podcasters, and again, it's within the realm of possibilities.

We tend to like to say that *work is not my life*, but the reality is that *we work with our life.* There is no separation. If you run a business, you think about your business most of the time. If you are hungry in your career, you are going to be spending the extra time to improve upon your craft. Careers and businesses are passions, and when mixed with podcasting, it's a highly interesting and powerful concoction.

At the time of this writing, the overall podcast search engine machine needs much refining. I am very confident, at some point in time, there will be a pseudo podcast google, offering advanced and precise search features, hopefully making it easier to get found. It can be difficult to get found, but many in the industry are working hard on optimizing and fixing this problem. It seems, right now, that the best way is to distribute and share the podcast in as many places as possible. The more, the better; especially in the places where your prospects are likely to be, or visit. It can feel like a job on its own, sharing your podcast on social media, podcast directories, pay per click advertising, etc. Add this to an existing lead generation process. In time, you will discover what will, and what will not, work for you.

Let's not forget about the fun of podcasting as an added layer of enjoyment to your business. You may decide to podcast for business but won't be able to avoid the fun of it. We all need fun and laughter, especially since we work so hard and make countless sacrifices. I have provided all of the proof that the process itself has the capability to add many forms to your personal success, but again, our lives are not divided two ways: work and real life. Be happy, and add the podcasting to your business.

Just remember that if you do this, don't bite off more than you can chew. If you run a successful business, then you have likely mastered the art of delegation. Treat the podcast this way as much as possible. There are a large number of editors and producers out there. Depending on what you envision, there are a number of resources to utilize. If you need a referral, just ask me.

There are no rules. Use your creativity. Bells and whistles are not required. It can be as easy as using only your voice in the podcast, with no music, nor intro or outro. I am a big fan at keeping it simple. When I hear elaborate productions, I think that a lot of money has been spent. That's okay, but it's not something that I value as a listener.

Know your prospects, what they value and need, and give it to them for free. Stand out, and show them how unique and special you and your business are. Have fun doing so, learn more about your industry, and implement the podcast as a content marketing strategy.

Ways to Begin to Monetize a Podcast

Monetization is often in the minds of podcasters. I am often asked, "How do I make money with my podcast?" There are a number of strategies that can be utilized. I don't go into too much detail, but if this is new to you, then at least it will give you a basic beginning.

Sponsorships & Advertisements

Options can be: sponsor your own show with your own business, or charge a company for podcast episode time. If you have listened to *The Podcaster's Life,* you will hear me read a 30-second ad on my coaching services, at http://podcasterscoach.com. My business sponsors the show, which is true since my income pays for the recording space, software, microphones, and audio hosting. It allows me to explain a service to my listeners, without needing or trying to sell myself during my interviews.

The other way to do it is to reach out to businesses or podcast advertising companies, and sell them your airtime. Sponsorship and advertising are a hot part of the podcast industry. A number of companies have found the benefit and reward to placing advertisements on podcasts. I believe that the demand is so big that there aren't enough qualified podcasters actively trying to get sponsors.

Yes, that sounds crazy, but there is a reason for this, and it's called podcast statistics. Podcasts must have great numbers to reap the rewards of sponsors. A few hundred downloads per episode simply will not suffice. One needs tens of thousands to make a substantial dent.

If you search for podcast advertising companies, you'll often find all of the information (that you need to know) is on their websites. You might even find an online calculator that will give you an idea of the type of money you can earn. As of this day of writing, I calculated that 30 seconds of air time (at the beginning of your podcast) would earn you a minimum of $3000 for one year, if you have 10,000 listeners, and you produce a weekly show.

Patrons & Premium Content

Another area of monetization, which is on the rise, is developing a fan base that will donate money to your show for access to premium content, and sometimes not. There is a leading website that you can search for that will give you the platform and space to do this. You simply post bonus content, and your patrons will be able to consume it with a monthly donation. The company will take a small fee from the donations, but the podcast community does not seem to mind this. Many are very successful at it, and some earn $5,000–$10,000 a month. These are the podcasts with a large, devoted fan base.

I've recently discovered that a podcast hosting company is offering the same type of service to their customers. I've also seen a few podcast websites that use a PayPal donate button, with a monthly subscription option. There are fees involved for both these alternatives.

Affiliate Marketing

Podcasters can join a company's affiliate program, thereby allowing the podcast host to earn a commission on products that are sold through their podcast, website, or other means. The company provides a special identifying URL, which tracks the origins of the sale. Commission rates vary, but some can be very generous.

It seems to be very easy to get accepted into affiliate programs. Once you get accepted, you can create your own customizable link, which redirects to the affiliate link, and then creates a spot/commercial for your website, talking about the product while sharing your URL link.

Ultimately, it depends on your goals and your listeners. Would people care to listen to an ad in exchange for a free, value-driven podcast? Probably not. There seems to be an understanding from the podcast listener who realizes that the podcast host is trying to earn income with their time.

The podcaster must remain true to their values and, if sponsorship, advertisements, and affiliate marketing are involved, they should align to the goals of the program, and definitively not chase away potential subscribers.

Forget About a Blog on Your Resumé – Add a Podcast Instead

Back in my head-hunting and recruiting days, I constantly heard the industry gurus giving advice on blogs for the resumés. Admittedly, when I provided career coaching back then, I would mention that it could be a tool to get a *candidacy* to stick out. It made sense at the time: write a blog about your industry (and career) and give prospective employers the opportunity to see your dedication and desire for your work. Put it at the top of the resumé, and make it very easy for your future manager to find and read your content.

I am not a big fan of blogs, and I rarely will read one. I just don't have the time. If I sit down and take some time to read, I'd rather get a book and hold it in my hand. I listen to podcasts all the time because I can listen as I move around, and when I am on the go.

Podcasts can, and do, replace blogs, or they can greatly enhance one. Podcasts have a simplicity to them that makes them incredibly effective. I don't think there is anything wrong with putting the podcast episode on top of the blog, which could just be a transcript of the actual podcast episode. Remember, no rules.

On a good resumé, the candidate will place their LinkedIn profile URL with their contact information. LinkedIn is a business networking social media website. Professionals seeking a move or career change will try to tell a story on their profile, and highlight their achievements. It's essentially an online resume for the job seeker, which can offer more than a word document.

Podcasts are versatile. A resumé, which has a professional looking and sounding podcast, will trump the other CVs. Hiring managers may only look at a resume for 30 seconds. They may give equal time to a LinkedIn profile. If they listen to the start of your podcast, and if you sound pleasant, they will give you more of their time. You hook them in with your professionalism, demeanor, and personality.

You can simply embed your best podcast episode on your LinkedIn profile, use your podcast hosting profile page, or create a simple Wordpress website that features your podcast, resumé, and your blog, if you have one.

The goal is to come across as an industry thought leader. Interview your peers, your partners, or anyone else that you admire in the industry. Create a podcast environment that is warm and friendly, and you will make strong connections with the people who give you their time.

You need podcast cover art. Take a professional image, and have a graphic artist give it a media shine. If a job seeker comes across looking like a *celebrity* podcaster, he or she makes a great impression. Humans cannot help judging others instantly. I've seen it so many times when it comes to hiring others. I have spent countless hours getting to know my candidates, and having been in a staffing professional in the industry, I became a very good judge of character and what made the best employees. But for one reason or another, if a candidate fumbled somehow at the very beginning stages of the interview process, it would be seen as a red flag, thus making it harder to get the job offer. Job seekers do not want to be holding any red flags!

Forget about faking a podcast for a job: it will ruin your reputation, and make future jobs very difficult to obtain. If you love your work, go for it! Having a regular podcast on your career and industry will show your uniqueness. You learn from others, you teach yourself, and you share your knowledge with your listeners from the industry. Perhaps it puts you into a mentorship role for those who listen, and want to be just like you.

The Full Time Podcasting Profession

There are people out there who make a living doing their own podcast, and working on other podcasts. Some earn enough money from their own show, having developed a huge listener base with sponsorship and advertising revenue from their programs. Others use their podcast as the center of an income stream, while offering additional podcast related products and services for sale. There are a handful of the earlier adopter podcasters who have worked long and hard to get to where they are today. The advantage of starting early is a strong reputation through experience, and the number of podcast episodes. Of course, being personable, having the desire to help others, and maintaining the passion for podcasting plays a big part in successfully running their podcast businesses. Like myself, and most others, when you start podcasting, you will probably stumble upon the big name podcasters first, and they will set a very good example, if you keep listening to them. They did for me, and I am pleased to tell you that I have had a positive experience with these podcast professionals, after I became *The Podcaster's Coach.*

What I am seeing more frequently now are podcasters becoming producers and editors. As the number of podcasts rise, the demand for help increases. It would seem that either you will like editing your podcast, or you dislike it. Those who are in disfavor of editing either spend time doing what they don't love, or they enjoy their life, and delegate the editing to someone else. It is becoming much easier to find a small business podcast editing service.

This is leading people into full time podcast related occupations. I have heard of podcasters getting involved in a niche industry, becoming known as a *podcaster*, and prompting their business peers to seek out their advice or help. Opportunities arise, and then, before long, due to the new stream of income, a decision has to be made: find time, somehow, to continue podcasting, or cut back on editing revenue. Steve Stewart is a wonderful example of this. He is an amazing editor, producer, and teacher.

I see both full-time and part-time podcast production companies and consultants popping up. Some continue to podcast, work a couple of part-time jobs (one of which being podcast editing), or simply put their own podcast on hold. Putting a podcast on hold is something that the podcaster has full control over. There is nothing stopping a podcaster to go on hiatus and return years later. Once the podcast returns with some form of regularity, listeners may return, or new ones will be had.

New editing clients are often found on Facebook in the podcast groups, meet ups, and conferences. All it takes are a handful of clients to get a full-time business off the ground. There are no *Podcast Editing Schools* that offer certifications that I have heard of, so it seems to be a level playing field. Mind you, those who are experienced will have the upper hand through their own podcast production, but this is just the way it goes—practice makes perfect. Perfection does not exist, but you know what I mean.

It's very exciting that someone can learn how to edit a podcast well, and start a new business. Thousands of dollars are not required to spend on a degree or diploma. Eventually, someone will start a *school*, but it could take decades before a degree or diploma becomes necessary for someone who edits podcasts. It reminds me of the recruiting and staffing profession. Recruiters do not go to school to become recruiters. They just happen to find themselves in the field one day. If they are any good at it, a very attractive income will follow. College degrees don't often matter in recruiting. All it takes is a private business owner to spot potential in someone, and give them their opportunity to start.

Right now, developing a podcast production portfolio, and having an aptitude for business, can be all it takes to get a new business off the ground. Every new business needs many hours, many sales attempts, and a break here and there.

If you are craving entrepreneurship, and love the creative elements to the podcast medium, then you can successfully transition into making a living through podcasts. The amount of time varies and, of course, depends on your drive, vision, and talent.

Podcasts as a Business Relationship Builder

As a business owner, in my previous businesses, I found it difficult to approach people when I didn't have enough reason. I wanted to connect with them, but I didn't know how to call them on the phone and ask them to talk to me. My thoughts were always, "They think I will try to sell them."

I would connect with people on LinkedIn, which was mostly safe to do, and I would either ask them, via LinkedIn message, if they were interested in talking, or I would warm call them, using LinkedIn as an excuse for the phone call. In retrospect, this was a poor strategy, and I didn't do this often, due to difficulty and poor results.

Your podcast *is* enough reason to reach out to someone in your industry, for both your career and your business.

It could look like this:

"Hello, my name is Alexander, and I am the host of the Business Marketing Mastermind Podcast. I have admired your work; am I interrupting you?"

"I have a minute; how can I help you?"

"I produce a successful show, with a worldwide audience, which focuses on thought leaders and influencers. I know about you through (insert here), and would like to invite you onto my program, where we can talk about you, promote your business, and provide the opportunity to offer advice for others in the industry. I suspect that you have so much that you can give to someone who wants to listen to your message. This would be a very easy process....."

It need not be more elaborate than this. Create your own script and reach out. You are calling and making someone feel special. Most of us love to talk about ourselves and help others. A podcast is an excellent way to do something of value. Yes, you are asking for someone's time, but if you make them understand how easy it can be, you will put them at great ease. It's as easy as jumping on Skype, or using a premium online interview recording service to capture your interviews.

As a business owner, it allows you deeper engagement with people in your industry. This is a great way to form new relationships and become a connector. The more people you know and network with, the more referrals you can make. The more you try to help others, the more others will try to help you.

Obviously, you don't call up your competitors and ask them to be on your podcast. You are in full control to create a safe space. You can reach out to potential partners, or those who you wish to learn from, who could help grow your business. If there is something that I really want to learn for my business, I call someone who knows much more than me, and it allows me to ask questions for the podcast interview. It's practically free mentorship for you and the people who follow and trust you.

You decide what works for you. You won't develop relationships with everyone you interview. I have not. Building a strong rapport is not possible with everyone, especially if they enter the interview with their guard or wall up in front of them; but if the relationship will not flourish, then at least you have created content to share, learned something new that you can try, and have made the interviewee feel good that they've been heard and understood. I end my show with a comedy segment, and my guests always leave feeling happy. Perhaps our personalities don't mingle with perfection, but at the very least, we shared good moments together. The possibility for a referral still exists in this situation.

Businesses should have a podcast. Small business owners, consultants, or solopreneurs should definitely podcast. The benefits far outweigh the costs. If you've been reading, and not skipping ahead, you already know about all of the amazing personal successes that can emerge through the process of podcasting. Business success is well within your range too.

Bonus
Podcaster Successes

"If you're dedicated to your community, it will be dedicated to you." – Robert Kiyosaki

I have met and created friendships with so many podcasters. The podcasters in this section have written short essays about podcasting success that has come into their lives in different ways. They provide some proof of what I have been trying to convey. As an additional **bonus**, please visit http://www.thebookonpodcasting.com, for one on one interviews with these podcasters, for additional content relating to their contributions in this chapter.

Overcoming the Imposter Syndrome 1% at a Time!
By Rob O'Donohue

I have a confession to make! I had never listened to a single podcast until late 2012. Sure, I had heard of a *podcast* but didn't really know what it was. *Isn't that just the same as radio?* I remember thinking! So, I decided to do a bit of digging into what these podcasts were all about. I'm not sure if someone had recommended one to me, or if the curiosity got the better of me, but I downloaded the Apple Podcast App (since then it has become a pre-installed app on the iPhone). By luck, not design, I stumbled across a podcast called, *Stuff You Should Know*. It had me at hello, or maybe at sho*uld know*. I remember vividly, listening to an episode while out for a 5km run, and I was hooked. Not just by this episode (I recall it was about the Berlin Wall) but more about the possibilities that I had available to me with podcasts. I had the opportunity to learn on the run, literally. I quickly realized that I had a mobile university in my ears, and it was, for the most part, free!

Fast forward to late 2016. As I continued to enjoy listening or consuming shows, I was still struck by the fact that many of my friends, or people I'd talk with, were unaware of the value that podcasts could bring. These folks were missing out! So, with some blind optimism, I started to investigate what I needed to do to create one myself, switching roles from consumer to producer, with the bold simple vision of creating a podcast that could help others learn, improve, and grow through the stories of others. This was my fledgling idea and was enough to get me started!

While this was a very exciting time, figuring out everything and anything I needed to do to pull this off, it was also a period where I felt paralyzed with fear. I remember (and still hear it regularly but much less) the negative self-talk raging. The questions coming up, to name just a few, were something like, *"Who do you think you are to create a podcast?" "You're a nobody." "What do you have to share?" "Who's going to listen to you?"* I'm probably keeping the language extra clean here. My inner gremlin has a colourful turn of phrase.

I've since learned that this is commonly known as **the imposter syndrome**! Well, ironically enough, thanks to the power and insights I gleamed from listening to podcasts that talked about this condition, I pushed through, felt the fear, and did it anyway.

Right & Left Brain in Action

Over the months that followed, I got it done. Firstly, I spent a lot of time getting clear on my **Why**. This took a lot of right brain work, getting clear on the purpose, vision, and mission. That's where the *1% Better* idea became clear. My aim was, and is, to create a show where every episode has the best content I can put together, and consistently provides listeners with insights, tools, and tips to help them get a little bit better. I'm a poor man's Tim Ferriss, if you will, with *slightly* more hair. J (Tim, if you're reading this, I hope your stoic view of the world will see this as a joke!)

With the **Why** clear, I then focused on the **How** and the **What**. I put a detailed plan together. My background is in project management. This helped hugely. Setting a **BHAG** (Big Hairy Audacious Goal) can be the easy part. Implementing it is what normally gets in the way. Setting the launch date was key! Telling others about it held me accountable to myself! I recall, as the project gained momentum, and I started to record my first interviews, my confidence grew. I was learning so much—about production, editing, interviewing, and most importantly, myself.

Then, in early March, 2017, one week ahead of schedule, after many long hours, and definitely lots of sweat, a few tears (I can't recall if there was any blood spilt, other than pricking my finger to check glucose levels.), and definitely after learning to overcome the embarrassment of the sound of my own voice, I launched my first set of shows. It was out in the public domain. It felt good. Another syndrome, which my boss at work liked to call *perfection being the enemy of good enough,* was strong during this time too. But the momentum was fierce, and the date was set, so it was time to go-live. Waiting for it to be perfect was not an option.

My original goal for the show was to do thirty in 2017. I ended the year with fifty. The journey had lead me to chat with world champions, world record holders, magicians, entrepreneurs, a person with clairaudience (look it up), a social media strategist, and one of Ireland's best-known chefs (thanks Neven). That's just to call out a few. With one hundred hours of content released, I had learned so much about topics such as business, start-ups, meditation, mindfulness, developing habits, morning routines, and even people's earliest memories. It's been an awesome experience.

Lessons Learned & Success

I started out this podcast voyage with a few personal goals in mind: give something back to the podcast world, which has helped me learn and keep fit over the last few years. By devouring hours of podcast content, I believe I have developed new habits and practices, which have made me more confident, and more willing to push through fears and set BHAGs for myself. I've confronted the imposter syndrome, head- on, by putting the content out there. What once was a loud voice inside my head, is now hardly audible at all. All this shows that if you set the goal, work out a plan to get there, be resilient, and stick the course, you can achieve it. Whatever *IT* is. It's a simple enough message to write, and much harder to execute, but it can be done.

In my performance coaching work, one of the tools I find the simplest, yet more powerful, is the ***Action Learning Cycle***. Taking **Action** to set up my own show has continued that **Learning Cycle** for myself, and moved things to the next level. In parallel, I've made connections with people I would never have otherwise. I've also been able to share these stories with thousands of others across the globe, and received emails from folks who have benefited from hearing the struggles and victories of others. And maybe, in some ways, they have become that 1% better, as a result.

In one of the episodes, a guest turned the success question that I ask, back on me. What is success for me? I didn't have to think too much. In that moment, the conversation I was having with the guest *was my success*. I was taking action and learning simultaneously. It was aligned to my *why, how,* and *what*.

Rob O'Donohue
AKA Rob of the Green
Rob@Robofthegreen.ie
www.robofthegreen.ie
Host of The 1% Better Podcast - Shared stories & practices that make you 1% Better 99% of the time!

Finding the Truth in Your Own Voice
By Steven Pacheco

There is some indefinable compulsion at our core, on a very human level, to help those around us. Some may call it a spiritual calling, though for me, it has always been about the reality of acknowledging someone's pain, and wanting to alleviate it. Initially, the podcast wasn't about helping others, at least not in that pure sense. I am fascinated by unsolved cases, and I wanted to spend my time talking about them. I thought, sure, perhaps I can shake something loose, or bring out a piece of evidence that has been overlooked, and maybe something will come of it, but it wasn't until I began doing the show that I discovered the power of my platform, and the ability I possessed to help others. A podcast, which began about unsolved cases, slowly transformed, and today, I do my best to focus on the victim over the suspects, and the family over the circumstances.

I deal with missing persons and unsolved murders, and questions without answers, which haunt the families and everyone who cared about the victims. As someone who has lost loved ones, I cannot imagine the depth of their pain in losing someone and not knowing what happened, or why, or who was responsible. That utter lack of closure leaves the wound unhealed, and I cannot deny that I feel an overwhelming compulsion to want to provide them with compassion. I can't solve the cases for them, but I can bring them back into the light, and do my best to keep the memory of their loved ones alive. The list of names is incredibly long, and for many, they feel frustrated that their loved one has been forgotten, or often times ignored by a media system that is based on ratings and not emotions. I have the ability to feature victims who haven't gotten the attention they deserve, and I do my best to focus on those cases that haven't been splashed all over the headlines.

There is a certain sense of selfishness about it. Doing something for others, reaching out and shining the light on a specific name, while it draws attention to the case and revitalizes interest, it also makes me feel good. It's comforting to be able to offer something back, and even if all you can do is resurrect a name that has been lost to time, it's more than what was being done yesterday. Imagine all the times in your life when you needed a helping hand or a comforting word. There is a certain wonder when someone reaches out, even in the smallest way. You don't need to change the world for someone, but to dedicate your time and heart to something that is near and dear to them can change everything. The greatest gift of hosting a podcast isn't in popularity or fame; it's in your ability to make someone else feel like they're not alone. I began as a listener, and it was that sense of comfort and unity that I wanted to be able to give back to.

It can be challenging to spend countless hours of the day researching, writing, and talking about incredibly painful situations—to submerge myself into the desperation and anguish of loss and the unknown— but what I feel reading about a case is nothing compared to what the family experiences in the time afterward. I can't take that burden from them, but I can attempt to share in it and allow them to know that they are not alone in this, and that there are others who care and wish to help in any way that they can. I've been contacted by family members of victims who have thanked me for discussing their loved one's story, and I can't begin to describe how it feels to know I've helped, even if only to lighten the load for a moment. The greatest thing you can do, I believe, is to help carry someone else's pain.

The world of technology is still, in many ways, an unexplored frontier. In a world where technology is ever expanding, we often find that those new methods of communication, which should bring us closer together, can actually divide us further. Podcasting offers the ability to bridge that gap, to reach out to others, and make genuine connections. Even though, for me, it began about curiosity and the unknown, it has become a platform to give a voice to those unable to speak for themselves, and a way to shine a light into the darkness of those who have been left behind without answers.

Steven Pacheco
Host of Trace Evidence – a true crime podcast focused on missing persons and unsolved murders.
TraceEvidencePod@gmail.com
Trace-Evidence.com

Doing it My Way: Podcasting as a Way to Becoming a Global Leader

By Bunmi Akinnusotu

The foreign policy sector is difficult to enter. Often, professionals in this space have family connections or military experience to gain access. If you have neither, programs like Study Abroad, Peace Corps, or Unpaid Fellowships are other avenues for breaking into the field. From there, you're most successful when you become an expert on an issue (e.g. terrorism) and/or region of the world. I've always remained abreast of foreign policy issues by volunteering with organizations that have some global footprint, and through my own personal study by reading magazines such as the Economist or Foreign Policy. I also went so far as to get two advanced degrees that I thought would catapult my career into the foreign policy space and, subsequently, obtaining the institutional prestige to validate what I know. I took the Foreign Service Officer test three times, and only progressed as far as the personal narrative portion before being rejected. While I was trying unconventional paths to break into the sector, I was unknowingly building a large network of experts in the foreign policy space. Ironically, I finally received an opportunity to work on international issues while serving in the Obama Administration. Finally, I thought, I had both the network and career experience to secure a position at a think tank, non-profit organization, or consulting firm. After the end of the Administration, it was clear to me: I still had more work to do, to finally stick the landing.

Washington D.C. is a competitive town. Not only are the jobs more or less the same, but so are the job seekers. Everyone has multiple advanced degrees from the same prestigious universities. Everyone knows of, and has connections to, the organizations, congressional leaders, or companies working in their area of interests. Everyone knows that 70% of jobs in DC are NOT posted publicly. And sadly, there's an unspoken understanding that in order to appear as the best candidate, everyone conveniently exaggerates the truth of what they've accomplished in previous roles. It's not uncommon to scratch your head in wonder as you learn who was hired and who was not. When I ended my tenure in the Administration, I knew all of this, but I didn't know the potency until I began interviewing, and was turned down for seemingly perfect opportunities. I have not yet figured out the key to success in Washington, or what people are saying in interviews that is so much better than what I am saying. But I do know that launching my podcast has opened more doors, and demonstrated further evidence of my commitment to foreign relations.

My long-term career goal is to become America's first Nigerian-American Ambassador. From what I've been told, there is no roadmap for becoming an Ambassador, particularly a politically appointed one. However, Ambassadors have certain qualities: they are bridge builders; they are social and cultural chameleons, and can fit in with diverse groups; they are curious and have a unique ability to view the world from others' perspectives. And most importantly, as the President's representative abroad, they operate with the utmost professionalism and humility. I haven't quite mastered all of this. Through my radio program and podcast, *"What in the World?"* I am a lot closer. The show has also been a useful conversation starter during job interviews; and particularly because I don't fit the profile of the older, white, male, Yale *foreign policy expert,* interviewers seem more intrigued by my career background, and also how I have used the podcast to explore American foreign policy. More than anything, this show has boosted my confidence, which had been challenged by a storm of rejections and a parade of disappointments that come with the job search. In a town full of uniform resumes and *looks, "What in the World?"* helps me offer something unique to potential employers, and the show demonstrates how serious I am about my long-term goals. Often, my guests, friends, and strangers share how impressed they are that I took an idea from concept to action. Apparently, in this town, people talk a big game but accomplish little. I have no doubt that someday, someone will recognize that this show reflects the type of foreign policy leaders America needs, as well as news explaining what in the world America is doing abroad. Until then, I will continue to grow as a podcaster, connect Americans to foreign policy in a way that's relevant, and hone the skills I need to achieve my dream of becoming an Ambassador.

Bunmi Akinnusotu
Creator & Producer
whatintheworldpod2017@gmail.com
whatintheworldpodcast.com
"What in the World?" **makes foreign policy understandable and relevant to ordinary Americans, and amplifies the voices of experts who are women and people of color.**

Bridging The Gap With a Father & Son Podcast
By Dave Lee

When I tell people I have been podcasting with my father, Steve, there are typically one of two responses: 1) That's amazing! Or, 2) Wow, I could never do that! For me, it's the former.

So, how did it all start? Back in 2007, Steve took a job, five hours north of where his family was located. In an effort to stay connected, my brother Mike and I would log on to Skype to chat about the week, work, and family. Inevitably, the conversation drifted toward technology, as Steve and Mike worked as IT professionals. At some point in time, Steve hit record without us knowing, and later sent the audio file, saying, "Guys, I say we start a podcast!" The rest is history, and we've been podcasting together for ten years now.

Steve is a proud Air Force veteran, serving 21 years. I grew up watching my father receive several temporary duty assignments that displaced him from the family. Adding the typical demands of serving in the Armed Services, time was a bit limited with the family. Civilian life brought about a new challenge as he began running his own Internet service company, and travelling worldwide with IBM. Despite that, the family always respected the call of duty, and relished moments when we came together. As we have transitioned to our busier adult lives, podcasting every Monday night has become a very meaningful event for me. We have a genuine bond over our moments of recording. Knowing that every minute we record is a minute of time we spend together, in some respects, makes up for lost time. Not only do we debate, banter, and discuss technology, we also debate, banter, and discuss personal issues and podcasting ideas.

A major component of a successful relationship is vulnerability. In the case of podcasting with my father, we have seen each other at our lowest and our highest, at our worst and best, at our most excited and most stressed, and at our most creative and most stagnant. We openly share our philosophies on what works and what doesn't. We openly critique each other's ideas to create better content. Many focus on downloads and income when it comes to measuring the success of their podcast. My father and I have redefined that definition while podcasting. The process of growing our podcast together, building relationships, and honing our craft, speak to our success. Because of that, our relationship has flourished.

Growing up, we hit the road in the family van and headed to Texas and Arizona. Those long drives are precious family memories. Our travels today have taken us to Las Vegas, Chicago, Orlando, Los Angeles, and other destinations, to attend and cover podcast and technology conferences. Steve's incentive to hit record has created new memories that have been etched into our history books. With space between us and busy lives distracting us, we always find podcasting to be a common ground that binds us together.

Dave Lee
Podcaster, The Waves of Tech
thewavesoftech@gmail.com
Co-Founder, International Podcast Day
https://internationalpodcastday.com/
dave@internationalpodcastday.com

Global Platform, Local Focus
By Ian Farrar

The world of podcasting has provided a gateway to the world for podcast hosts. I still find it exciting reviewing the listener's stats, and finding out that I have subscribers in the most obscure outposts of the world.

World domination is often a dream for podcasters, but we must not forget the network that we have grown closer to home. Likeminded subscribers in your local region, who relate to your content, are extremely open to meet ups. This can easily be arranged with a little help from local networks.

Local agencies, chambers of commerce, partnerships, industry bodies, etc. are tasked to collaborate and bring value to their memberships and catchment. Membership managers are constantly planning the next event with a goal of bums on seats, excitement, and doing things a little differently to the competition, thereby adding new members. You, the podcast host, have something different to draw the crowds.

My show is a business show where I interview entrepreneurs/ leaders/founders, etc. An interview style show can work really well in a live environment. I am fortunate to live in a region where technology and innovation is on the tip of everyone's tongue. This provides me with an inexhaustible supply of exciting business leaders to share with the world.

Working with a local partner can provide you with a venue, an email list, and a willing colleague to help arrange the details. Local businesses will also be interested in sponsorship opportunities if they can raise their banner, have a brief intro with the audience, and achieve their logo and link on your website (these links can flow straight into their SEO strategy).

Recording the podcast live in front of an audience not only provides your fans a chance to meet and interact with you; it allows you a chance to win over new subscribers who enjoyed the event. It gives you the opportunity to hand out stickers, talk about your business, and ask for reviews. Social media will blow up on the day with your unique hash tags, and people in the audience sharing pictures and comments. I noticed an increase in followers, likes, shares, and podcast downloads.

Following the live episode, a networking event with beer and pizza is a great way to mingle with attendees, and get firsthand feedback of how the event was and how your podcast is performing. Partnering with a local photographer can provide some pictures of the event to share on social media, and the photographer will enjoy being exposed to your audience. I gained some great pictures that I've used on my website and my social media profile pictures. Pictures such as these can really help add gravitas to your personal brand.

Of course, recording the audio for your podcast subscribers isn't the only medium to utilize. Why not capitalize and take along some basic equipment, and live stream through the various social media channels. This content is great for the people who couldn't make it, and can also be shared post show for people catching up.

From recording my first live podcast episode, I immediately had two further offers to record at events. I am hoping to continue to grow these live events with an increased audience size, and take it to the bigger stages. This may lead to monetizing the live episodes

In summary, ensure to take advantage of your network and personal brand; you have a fantastic opportunity to tap into, right there on your doorstep. Your podcast will grow by word of mouth if you are physically in the same room as them, adding amazing value.

Ian Farrar
Host: Industry Angel Business Podcast
Founder & CEO: Far North
https://mrfarrar.com/
Industry Angel is the top-ranking Business Podcast. We hear from Business Leaders, Entrepreneurs, Social Influencers….even the odd Adventurer or two!

What Podcasting Does For Me
By Joseph Fanning

Well, there are a few things. First, as all podcasters are, I am ego driven. I love the satisfaction of knowing that even if only ONE person is listening and being entertained, it's worth it to me, and of being able to identify with them on that level. It's a very personal experience as there is no live audience in front of you. People listen at different times, days, and for different reasons. Although a live audience may give you more of an immediate *rush*, I happen to like the solitary, personal aspect of it all, for the listener. Even if they're in groups, it's still like a local community to each *cell*. Think of sports. There are plenty of fans of each particular team, who don't know each other, but they have a common bond.

Also, I suffer from bipolar disorder, so this is a form of therapy for me as well. I can vent, get angry, be depressed, whatever...and it helps *cleanse* me mentally by putting it out there. It's an audible diary of sorts—a purging—a way for me to not only release my tensions and concerns, but to satisfy my mental needs by knowing that people actually like hearing me do it. When you can turn a crippling illness into a positive, in ANY way, it's a victory to be sure, especially if it benefits others as well as you.

It also brings my family closer together. By that, I mean that when my brother and I do our show (he is my co-host), we obviously bond for that hour and a half to two hours, but we then have dinner with our mother afterward. My brother is an *out of sight, out of mind* type of person, and before the show, my mother wouldn't see him as much. She hates the show but loves that it brings her first born to the house more often. We also have relatives who live far away and, when they hear us, they say it's like sitting at the Thanksgiving dinner table.

Another thing is that it keeps me connected. I mean, I do a comedy oriented show, but it's mostly a political/current events type show, so it forces me to stay informed. As painful as it is to have to listen to Trump clips over and over before final production, I feel it makes me a better citizen, as I am in the loop as far as news and politics go. Quite often, along with mental illness, there is addiction. I was a drug addict for many years. I floated on the edge of society, not caring what was happening in the country or the world; so, staying on top of things these days not only serves its purpose as far as the podcast and keeping me sharp goes, it also reminds me of where I was—how I DIDN'T care because of my addiction—and no matter how frustrating it may be, it's a positive and not a negative.

I also love the audience interaction. I have actually become friends with a few listeners. What's great about that is how I can become a regular guy to them. They start out a little *star struck*, even though I'm a nobody, but if you admire someone, and they have a public platform, it's enticing to want to get to know them, and normal to be a little flustered upon initial contact. You become a part of their life as a result of their listening, and it makes their day when you actually just get down to earth and talk to them. I have been on the other end of that spectrum, as a fan who has met his idols, and it's pretty intense. I'm not on that same scale, but you get the point. I really don't ever want to be famous, but if I were, to whatever degree it is, I'd love and take pride in truly connecting with as many listeners as I can on a personal level. To make someone's day with a small gesture like a PM, email, phone call, social media interaction, or even having them as a guest on the show, is such a great reward. They give me as much joy as I give them, just by listening, identifying, and laughing with me.

Doing this show does more for me than anyone can ever know.

Joseph Fanning
Host of the Potentium Podcast
potentiumpodcast.com

Podcasting as a Tool For Improved Mental Health
By Michael Howie

Mental health issues are hard to talk about and, in my experience, hard to hear about. But being honest with myself and my audience about my generalized anxiety disorder, and the feelings of compassion fatigue I confront, challenges me to be a better podcaster, and a healthier person.

My mental health story isn't that remarkable: I had no trauma or *incidents* as a child, but I was always considered nervous, or a worrier. By the time I was hitting my adult years, it manifested into more significant physical issues, as well as affecting my ability to perform at school and work, and maintain relationships. Overtime, I got a variety of treatments, but it wasn't without personal cost: friendships, my first marriage, opportunities, and a significant amount of self-esteem were all lost along the way.

Today, I'm much healthier. I use a combination of medication and therapies, as well as making good choices for myself. A part of that is talking about myself and my mental health through my podcast. Though my show isn't about mental health, it does come up in two ways: my personal experiences with anxiety and how it impacts my views of whatever subject we may be covering, and compassion fatigue.

Also known as burnout, compassion fatigue is a common threat to animal advocates, healthcare workers, or anyone else who works in an industry that results in a great deal of emotional stress. I am extremely proud that in four full seasons of the show, I've covered compassion fatigue five times (not including a few webinars). And while I want to use the cliché that "if only one person is helped, I'll feel better," I can honestly say that I feel better, because I feel better.

Talking about mental health—whether it's my own struggle, or the daily grinds of compassion fatigue, or just regular stresses—makes me feel better. I feel good about myself, and my confidence and self-esteem grow when I listen to the conversations I've had about it on the show.

That said, it is a wonderful feeling when a listener says they've reached out for professional help, or are improving in their own mental health struggles after hearing me talk about my own.

Podcasting itself is also an avenue to explore emotional or difficult ideas in a safe manner: I can reach out and talk to ethics professors, and work through thoughts or concerns that have been affecting me negatively; I can get tips on how wildlife rehabilitators manage the stresses in their day-to-day lives; I can even talk to political leaders about finding hope in what often feels like hopeless situations.

I have found solace and support in podcasting, as well as growing my self-esteem and feelings of self-worth, in a medium that I'm able to share with likeminded individuals. Podcasting can't replace therapy, or medication, or self-care. But it can be a tool to improve mental health, and that's pretty amazing.

Michael Howie, a former award-winning journalist, is host of Defender Radio: the podcast for wildlife advocates and animal lovers.
TheFurBearers.com

The Foot of the Mountain
By Pavo

All podcasters have their reasons for starting their particular podcast. Maybe they want to just spend time talking about bad movies with friends once a week, or to celebrate things in their lives that they love, or to communicate to a wider audience something they feel may be interesting. I am guilty for creating a separate podcast for each of the previous reasons. When I decided it was time for me to try and lose weight (again!), I knew I needed to take a different approach. *The Foot of the Mountain* was born.

I have been overweight most of my life and have been on every diet that has been around. I needed to find a way to do it this time that made me accountable to others rather than just myself.

I was chatting to my wife while we were walking on a beach, on a short weekend away together, and rolled out the question, "Would it be possible to lose 1lb a week, for 100 weeks?" It felt like it was very doable. So, the idea was in my head, but it was how to do it that left me thinking. Anyone who knows me, knows that I love podcasts. I love listening to them, and I love making them. So it seemed a perfect fit. After a session of brain storming about what the podcast would be, and how it would work, I stumbled across the title. I thought, "Here I go, having to climb this mountain of losing weight again." I carried on sorting out the format, and once everything was settled in the head, I prepared for the first episode.

Now, the way I work, when recording podcasts, is that I nearly always under prepare. Some would say that's unprofessional or careless, but for me, and me alone, I like that feeling of unpredictability, not knowing what I'm going to say next, and being surprised about the words coming out of my mouth. If you listen to the first episode of TFOTM (and I'd love it if you did!), you'll hear that I start by reading a prepared piece on mic. Halfway through the read, I knew this didn't sound like me, so I just stopped, and started talking from the heart. To me, that's the essence of podcasting. It doesn't matter what subject you are talking about, or whether it's funny or not, or controversial or not—if it comes from the heart, it'll be fascinating to listen to.

One last point: after nearly five years of podcasting, I still have doubts when recording a podcast. I'll be sitting in my little converted shed, thinking, "What's the point? No one is listening!"

How wrong can you be? Modern technology is a wonderful thing, and your word can reach every corner of this glorious planet, and can touch people who are alone in ways you cannot imagine.

If you are only 1% interested in starting a podcast, then grab a computer, a mic, and a friend, and start recording. You won't be sorry. You'll catch the bug, and you'll be glad you did.

Pavo
The Foot of the Mountain – My quest is to lose 1lb a week, for 100 weeks, and my podcast is tracking my progress while also chatting to others at *the foot of their own mountain*.
footmountain@hotmail.com
www.footmountainpod.com

Podcasting as an Art Form
By Josh Naaman

I'm new to podcasting, but I'm not new to creating. My name is Josh Naaman, and I just launched a podcast, video, and book series, at the end of 2017, called *The Belief Books*. I created every aspect of my project, over the last two years, from traveling to interview guests, designing the logo and branding, creating the website, writing and recording the music, and learning how to podcast. I have been a creator for many years, but podcasting is one of the only mediums I've ever worked in that combines almost every artistic skill I've developed.

This has all been a wonderful, challenging, and enlightening journey; one that led me to meet Alexander Laurin, and led me to write these words in his book. When I was a guest on his show, this past December, he asked me if I thought podcasting was an art form. The answer was so easy and, obviously, "yes," to me. I hadn't thought about that specific question until then, but I knew very easily that I was creating and participating in a new form of art. You should listen to that episode, but here, Alexander let me expand on that question.

First, the answer is easy because of how loose the term *art* is. If you think about it, we can call just about anything *art*. It's inherently subjective. I didn't want to reference a dictionary definition for this, but it makes sense to deconstruct what we have defined art to be, before answering the question at hand.

"[Art is] the expression or application of human creative skill and imagination...producing works to be appreciated primarily for their beauty or emotional power."

Have you ever listened to a podcast? How many different kinds have you listened to? If you have listened to even just a few different podcasts, I think you have a good idea of what potential is out there, and the many skills it can take to produce just one episode, if not hundreds.

I have only been producing podcasts for about a year, but I've been listening to them for many years, and now, more than ever. There's vast talent, beauty, and emotional power in so many podcasts. From the visually stimulating episode, *Colors*, by Radiolab, to the suspenseful, investigative, two-part series, *Long Distance*, by ReplyAll, to the incredibly deep dissection of history, by Dan Carlin, to the socially provoking podcasts from Joe Rogan, Sam Harris, Seth Andrews, and Dave Rubin, podcasts are undoubtedly a diverse art form.

Josh Naaman
Host & Author
www.thebeliefbooks.com
beliefbooks@gmail.com
The Belief Books **is a new podcast, video, and book series, covering all topics about beliefs. The first chapters cover climate change denial, science, and faith.**

Keeping the Legacy Alive Through Podcasting
By Jesse Kahat

Inspiration is all around us. I've been consistently influenced and energized by the ocean of creations using audio out there. The podcasting community has caught me off guard in the most positive way, and I am constantly learning that there are very few limitations when it comes to the possibilities of experimentation in this medium. You can follow my podcast series, at thebeliefbooks.com, to see what I come up with in this special podcasting world.

Success is a funny concept; not only does everyone have a different definition of success, your personal definition of success can change at any point in time. If you would have asked me, at 18 years old, what my definition of success was, I would have said *being a Broadway star.* If you would have asked me at 25 years, it would have been *ballroom dance champion.* If you had asked me at 30, it would have been *VP of Sales at a multi-million dollar company.*

My definition of success (and everything else for that matter) was permanently altered following a phone call, on a November's day, in 2014. I'll never forget the tone of my mom's voice: it was soft and vulnerable, which was a departure from her normal chipper and witty tone. My mom was the strongest person I knew, and she was the person I called on for everything—advice, emotional support, laughs, strength—EVERYTHING. It was strange to hear her voice shake as she told me that the doctors had run some tests, and that she was most likely in for the worst news: cancer. The next couple of weeks were a blur of tests, tears, praying, pleading, hope, and despair. I thought if anyone could fight and beat cancer's ass, it would be my mom. Unfortunately, the fight wasn't a fair one, and it was revealed that she was in a terminal stage, with 6 to 24 months to live. Damn. Double Damn.

From that moment forward, the only thing that mattered was showing my mom how much she was loved, and how much of an impact she made on this world. She was so well loved and respected by everyone she interacted with on a regular basis, and gave so much of herself to so many people. I started to try and imagine how I could possibly go on without her guidance, wisdom, love, and support. More often than not, I would find myself thinking this would be impossible. I was terrified that once she was gone, I would lose my memories of her, my kids would forget about their grandma, and she would fade away, erasing everything she had accomplished.

On my first visit home since hearing the news, my mom sat my sister and me down at my sister's dining room table, and started talking about special things she wanted us to have after she passed away. If you have never had this conversation before, it is harder than you can possibly imagine. She mentioned a special necklace that she wanted me to have, and a few items for the kids. She said she wasn't sure what to do with her beautiful pearl necklace, and I told her I didn't want her pearls, just her pearls of wisdom. THAT was my lightning strike moment: my mom's pearls of wisdom were how I would be able to keep her legacy alive.

My mom was always spouting off little sayings and pearls of wisdom, and these were gems I didn't want to forget. Little tidbits of advice that would lead to me being my best self, and living my best life—these would be my key to keeping my connection with the woman who meant everything to me. I started by painting mini versions, which were visual representations of my favorite pearls of wisdom from her. This was a really therapeutic outlet for me to express my feelings in a creative way. It helped me get through her passing away 8 months into her treatment, and I wanted to share these with close friends and family, to help them remember her too. Since my sister and I live thousands of miles apart, and in different countries, a blog was the easiest way for me to share these with the world.

Alas, blogging was hard for me to keep up with consistently because it is very one-sided. What I really wanted was a way to unite other people who had lost their mom, and wanted to share her wisdom. After becoming obsessed with listening to podcasts, I started to wonder if this was a medium that would allow me to connect with others and share their stories. I decided to take the plunge, and I set a launch date for August 18, 2017, which would have been my mom's 68th birthday. When I set out to create a podcast, I had no idea if I would be able to find anyone to be a guest, or if anyone would want to listen, but it didn't matter. I saw my podcast as a way for me to share my mom's legacy with the world, and even if no one listened, it would be fun and therapeutic for me.

I am happy to say that people did want to be guests, and people did want to listen. Through podcasting, I have managed to forge those connections I was longing for, and met some really incredible people in the process. By talking about her and sharing her pearls of wisdom with others, I feel as though my mother lives on through me, which makes me happier than I could have thought possible. I do miss her every single day, but knowing that I still have a relationship with her, even though she is gone, is everything I needed. I feel like I am creating something that will live on even after I am gone, which is important for me to do for my kids. I encourage everyone to create something to leave behind for their loved ones, and as I say, on the *Pearls from My Mom* podcast, keep sharing to keep the legacy alive.

Jesse Kahat
Founder of Pearls from My Mom
www.PearlsFromMyMom.com
pearlsfrommymom@gmail.com
Pearls from My Mom **is a podcast dedicated to helping people, who have lost their moms, share their favorite stories and pearls of wisdom—sharing to keep the legacy alive.**

Final Words

Fulfillment, meaning, purpose, happiness, relationships, self-help, enjoyment, self-improvement, personal growth, career, business, and income are all components to the life of success. My very first podcast started off as fun; then I wanted to include it in my business. When I tried to do it, I couldn't. I could not add the pleasure of the podcast into the misery of being in a business that I did not like. The process of podcasting helped me make the firm decision to change my life. Creating *The Work Utopia Podcast,* ultimately, resulted in my self-therapy, healing, and discovery.

I spent my entire business life measuring my success from income alone. I did have many years of great financial success. I achieved more financial wealth than I ever thought I could possibly attain. Money and business success eventually became a *been there, done that* scenario. I completely ignored all of the other areas of life that could have sustained me or propped up happiness.

If you are already on this podcasting journey, and if you expand your definition of success, you will find a greater sense of contentment. In this day and age, money has become the measure of everything, it seems. I was born in the province of Quebec, where churches are ubiquitous. Society was very heavy Christian in the formation of the province. Now, the churches are turning into condominiums. Consumerism is the new religion. There is no purpose to be found in this system. It's all about *more* and *luxury* representing the good life. If you can't have *more,* or *luxury*, you're not successful?

You, the podcaster, or aspiring podcaster, do not need to accept a narrow definition of success. You can choose an expanded and enhanced version. Make the choice and use the tool—your podcast—to get it! You possess the strength and potential to be the successful person that you desire to be. Choices create the possibilities.

There is something very special about the podcaster. If you do it for your business, or career, or out of a passion, there exists a uniqueness that sets you apart from most of the other people in your life. I have thought that there were similarities between folklore and podcasts. Podcasts may not completely fit the most academic definition of folklore, but podcasts are filled with stories that we can use to learn and understand about the times, the lessons, and the lives of the period. Podcasts may be the new folklore— infused with technology.

You are a great creative force behind that microphone. The world can become a blank canvas for you at any time. Begin anew, let your voice be the brush, let the soul within become your companion in the space, and give yourself the time to practice and reflect on the words, energy, and potential about what you are capable of achieving. A most successful life is a happy life. It's the consistent feeling of doing good, helping others, having passion, and being heard.

My mission in life is to help 1,000,000 Podcasters. If I have helped you, please let me know. Please visit http://podcasterscoach.com/million to click the counter and leave a comment. Thank you.
-The Podcaster's Coach
#1MPodcasters